Ultimate Vegetable Side Dish Cookbook

Vegetables For Every Season & Occasion!

S. L. Watson

DEDICATION

To all those glorious vegetables we grow & eat every year!

CONTENTS

Introduction

We all know we need to eat more green vegetables. It is not always easy with a busy life and trying to feed the family what they will eat. This cookbook is full of family style recipes for spinach, broccoli, kale, turnip greens, green beans, asparagus, corn, tomatoes, squash and more. The recipes use everyday ingredients for easy vegetable meals and dishes for your family.

Recipes are great for holidays, everyday dinners, barbecue's, parties and more.

1 GREEN VEGETABLE SIDE DISHES

Vegetables are always a great side dish choice. Use a wide variety of vegetables to round out your meal. Most of the dishes are simple to prepare and tasty enough that even picky eaters will try them. Try to incorporate at least 1 green vegetable side dish into every meal.

Broccoli with White Wine

Makes 6 servings

1/4 cup olive oil
1 tsp. minced garlic
5 cups chopped fresh broccoli
1 1/2 cups dry white wine
1/2 tsp. salt
Black pepper to taste

In a skillet over medium heat, add the olive oil. When the oil is hot, add the broccoli and garlic. Stir constantly and cook for 3 minutes. Add the white wine and salt. Simmer for 2 minutes.

Place a lid on the skillet and reduce the heat to low. Simmer for 10 minutes. Remove the skillet from the heat and season to taste with black pepper.

Honey Mustard Veggies

This is one of my favorite ways to eat veggies and so easy too! The sauce works well with most vegetables and potatoes.

Makes 5 servings

1 lb. pkg. frozen broccoli, carrots & water chestnuts
2 tbs. light brown sugar
3 tbs. unsalted butter
2 tbs. honey
1 tbs. Dijon mustard
1/8 tsp. salt

In a sauce pan over medium heat, add the broccoli, carrots and water chestnuts. Cover with water and bring to a boil. Cook for 6 minutes or until the vegetables are tender. Remove the pan from the heat. Drain all the water from the vegetables and add to a serving bowl.

In a small microwavable bowl, add the brown sugar, butter, honey, Dijon mustard and salt. Stir until combined. Microwave for 1 minute or until the butter melts. Remove from the microwave and stir until combined. Pour the sauce over the vegetables. Toss until the vegetables are coated in the sauce. Serve hot.

Broccoli with French Sauce

Makes 8 servings

10 cups fresh broccoli, cut into bite size pieces
2 cups water
2 tbs. unsalted butter
2 tbs. all purpose flour
1 cup chicken broth
1/2 tsp. Worcestershire sauce
1/4 tsp. salt
1/8 tsp. black pepper
4 hard boiled eggs, sliced
1/2 cup sliced pimento stuffed green olives

In a large sauce pan over medium heat, add the broccoli and water. Bring to a boil and place a lid on the pan. Cook about 10 minutes or until the broccoli is tender. Remove the pan from the heat and drain all the water from the pan.

Place the broccoli in a serving dish and keep warm while you prepare the sauce. In a sauce pan over medium heat, add the butter. When the butter melts, add the all purpose flour. Stir constantly and cook for 1 minute. Add the chicken broth, Worcestershire sauce, salt and black pepper. Stir constantly and cook until the sauce thickens and bubbles. Remove the pan from the heat and pour the sauce over the broccoli. Place the hard boiled eggs and green olives over the top before serving.

Italian Style Broccoli

This is an excellent holiday or everyday side dish.

Makes 4 servings

1/3 cup finely chopped onion
1 garlic clove, minced
2 tbs. olive oil
1 1/2 lbs. fresh broccoli, cut into 2" spears
1/4 cup water
1/2 tsp. salt
1/4 tsp. chili powder

In a large skillet over medium heat, add the onion, garlic and olive oil. Saute for 3 minutes. Add the broccoli, water, salt and chili powder to the skillet. Stir until well combined.

Place a lid on the skillet. Cook for 10 minutes or until the broccoli is tender. Remove the skillet from the heat and serve.

Broccoli with Horseradish Sauce

Makes 6 servings

6 cups fresh broccoli florets
1/2 tsp. salt
3/4 cup sour cream
1/2 tsp. prepared horseradish
1 1/2 tsp. yellow prepared mustard
Pinch of paprika

In a sauce pan over medium heat, add the broccoli and salt. Cover the broccoli with water and cook about 8 minutes or until the broccoli is tender. Remove the pan from the heat and drain any water from the pan. Place the broccoli on a serving platter. Keep the broccoli warm while you prepare the sauce.

In the same sauce pan used to cook the broccoli, add the sour cream, horseradish and mustard. Stir constantly and cook only until the sauce is thoroughly heated. Remove the pan from the heat and spoon the sauce over the broccoli. Sprinkle the paprika over the top of the sauce.

Broccoli in Orange Sauce

Makes 6 servings

6 cups fresh broccoli florets
2 tbs. unsalted butter
2 tbs. all purpose flour
1/2 cup orange juice
1/2 tsp. grated orange zest
1/2 cup fresh orange sections
1/4 tsp. dried tarragon
1/4 tsp. salt
1/2 cup plain yogurt

Add the broccoli to a sauce pan over medium heat. Cover the broccoli with water and cook about 10 minutes or until the broccoli is tender. Remove the pan from the heat and drain all the water from the pan.

While the broccoli is cooking, make the sauce. In a sauce pan over medium heat, add the butter. When the butter melts, add the all purpose flour. Stir constantly and cook for 1 minute. Add the orange juice, orange zest, orange sections, tarragon and salt. Stir constantly and cook until the sauce thickens and bubbles. Remove the pan from the heat and stir in the yogurt.

Place the broccoli on a serving platter. Spoon the orange sauce over the broccoli and serve.

Orange Ginger Broccoli

Makes 4 servings

1 lb. pkg. frozen broccoli spears
1/2 cup water
1/4 tsp. dried thyme
1 orange, sliced
3 tbs. unsalted butter
1 tbs. honey
1/4 tsp. ground ginger

In a large skillet over medium heat, add the broccoli and water. Sprinkle the thyme over the broccoli. Place the orange slices over the broccoli. Place a lid on the skillet. Cook for 8 minutes or until the broccoli is tender. Remove the orange slices from the skillet and discard.

In a microwavable bowl, add the butter, honey and ginger. Microwave for 1 minute or until the butter melts. Remove from the microwave and stir until combined. Drizzle over the top of the broccoli. Toss until combined. Remove the skillet from the heat and serve.

Broccoli with Sesame Seeds

Makes 6 servings

3 tbs. vegetable oil
6 cups fresh broccoli florets
2 tsp. minced garlic
1/2 cup sliced water chestnuts
3 tbs. white wine
3 tbs. soy sauce
1/2 tsp. salt
1/2 tsp. granulated sugar
2 tbs. sesame seeds

In a skillet over medium high heat, add the vegetable oil. When the oil is hot, add the broccoli florets. Stir constantly and cook for 3 minutes. Add the garlic and cook for 2 minutes.

Add the water chestnuts, white wine, soy sauce, salt and granulated sugar. Stir frequently and cook for 6 minutes. Remove the skillet from the heat and sprinkle the sesame seeds over the top before serving.

Marinated Broccoli

Makes 8 servings

1 cup cider vinegar
1 tbs. fresh dill, minced
1 tbs. granulated sugar
1 tsp. salt
1 tsp. black pepper
1 tsp. garlic salt
1 1/2 cups vegetable oil
9 cups fresh broccoli florets

In a mixing bowl, add the cider vinegar, dill, granulated sugar, salt, black pepper, garlic salt and vegetable oil. Whisk until well combined. Add the broccoli and toss until the broccoli is coated in the marinade.

Cover the bowl and chill at least 8 hours before serving. Drain the marinade from the broccoli before serving.

Broccoli with Lemon Cream

Makes 6 servings

6 cups fresh broccoli, cut into bite size pieces
1 cup water
6 oz. pkg. cream cheese, softened
1/2 cup whole milk
1 tsp. grated lemon zest
1 tbs. lemon juice
1/2 tsp. ground ginger
1/2 cup slivered almonds
1 tbs. melted unsalted butter

In a sauce pan over medium heat, add the broccoli and water. Place a lid on the pan and cook about 8 minutes or until the broccoli is tender. Remove the pan from the heat and drain all the water from the pan.

Place the broccoli in a 11 x 7 baking dish. In a mixing bowl, add the cream cheese, milk, lemon zest, lemon juice and ginger. Stir until well combined. Spoon the sauce over the broccoli. Cover the dish with aluminum foil.

Preheat the oven to 350°. Bake for 15 minutes or until the sauce is bubbly. While the broccoli is cooking, add the almonds and butter to a small sauce pan over medium heat. Stir constantly and cook about 5 minutes or until the almonds are toasted. Remove the pan from the heat. Remove the baking dish from the oven. Remove the aluminum foil from the dish. Sprinkle the almonds over the top and serve.

Stir Fry Broccoli

Makes 6 servings

1/4 cup boiling water
2 tbs. soy sauce
1 tbs. dry sherry
1 tsp. granulated sugar
1/4 tsp. salt
1/4 cup peanut oil
4 cups fresh broccoli florets, cut into bite size pieces
1 onion, chopped

In a small bowl, add the boiling water, soy sauce, sherry, granulated sugar and salt. Whisk until combined.

In a skillet over high heat, add the peanut oil. When the oil is hot, add the broccoli and onion. Stir constantly and cook for 5 minutes. Reduce the heat to medium. Add the soy sauce dressing to the broccoli and toss until combined. Place a lid on the skillet and cook for 5 minutes. Remove the skillet from the heat and serve.

Roasted Broccoli With Orange Chipotle Butter

Makes 6 servings

24 oz. pkg. fresh broccoli florets
2 tbs. olive oil
1/4 cup unsalted butter, softened
2 tsp. grated orange zest
1 tsp. minced canned chipotle pepper in adobo sauce
1/2 tsp. salt

Preheat the oven to 450°. Add the broccoli and olive oil to a mixing bowl. Toss until the broccoli is coated in the oil. Spread the broccoli on a large baking pan. Bake for 15 minutes or until the broccoli is crisp tender. Remove the pan from the oven.

In a serving bowl, add the butter, orange zest, chipotle pepper and salt. Stir until combined. Add the hot broccoli to the bowl. Toss until the broccoli is coated in the butter. Serve hot.

Broccoli Carrot Supreme

Makes 8 servings

16 oz. pkg. frozen cut broccoli
6 carrots, peeled and cut into thin slices
1/4 cup chopped onion
2 tbs. melted unsalted butter
1/2 cup dry white wine
1 tsp. salt
1 tsp. dried thyme
1/8 tsp. black pepper
1 bay leaf
1/4 cup whipping cream
1/4 cup chopped pecans

In a sauce pan over medium heat, add the broccoli and 1 cup water. Bring to a boil and place a lid on the pan. Cook for 8 minutes or until the broccoli is tender. Remove the pan from the heat and drain all the water from the broccoli.

In a large skillet over medium heat, add the carrots, onion and butter. Saute for 5 minutes. Add the white wine, salt, thyme, black pepper and bay leaf. Place a lid on the skillet and reduce the heat to low. Simmer for 10 minutes or until the carrots are tender. Remove the bay leaf from the skillet and discard. Add the broccoli, whipping cream and pecans to the skillet. Stir until combined and cook until thoroughly heated. Remove from the heat and serve.

Bok Choy Broccoli Stir Fry

Makes 6 servings

2 tbs. vegetable oil
1 onion, thinly sliced
1/2 tbs. grated ginger root
2 garlic cloves, minced
1/2 tsp. salt
3 cups sliced fresh broccoli florets
7 cups chopped bok choy
2 tbs. lemon juice
1 1/2 tsp. granulated sugar

In a large skillet over medium high heat, add the vegetable oil. When the oil is sizzling, add the onion, ginger, garlic and salt. Stir constantly and cook for 2 minutes.

Add the broccoli and bok choy to the skillet. Stir constantly and cook for 1 minute. Add the lemon juice and granulated sugar. Stir constantly and cook for 4 minutes. Remove the skillet from the heat and serve.

Spinach with Mushrooms

Makes 4 servings

1 tbs. lemon juice
1 tsp. salt
1 tsp. granulated sugar
1/8 tsp. nutmeg
3 tbs. peanut oil
1 cup sliced fresh mushrooms
1 onion, chopped
1 garlic clove, minced
1 lb. fresh spinach, washed

In a small bowl, whisk together the lemon juice, salt, granulated sugar and nutmeg. In a skillet over high heat, add the peanut oil. When the oil is sizzling hot, add the mushrooms, onion and garlic. Stir constantly and cook for 3 minutes.

Add the spinach to the skillet. Stir constantly and cook for 3 minutes. Pour the lemon juice mixture over the spinach and vegetables. Stir until combined and remove the skillet from the heat.

Mexican Spinach

Makes 6 servings

3 pkgs. frozen chopped spinach, 10 oz. size
1 tbs. canola oil
1 cup chopped onion
1 garlic clove, minced
2 Anaheim chiles, roasted, seeded & minced
3 fresh tomatillos, roasted, husked & chopped

Add the spinach to a 5 quart slow cooker. In a large skillet over medium heat, add the canola oil. When the oil is hot, add the onion and garlic. Saute for 5 minutes. Add the chiles and tomatillos to the skillet. Saute for 4 minutes. Remove the skillet from the heat and add to the slow cooker. Stir until combined.

Set the temperature to low. Cook for 4 hours or until the spinach is tender. Stir before serving.

Baked Spinach Tomatoes

Makes 12 servings

12 ripe tomatoes
2 1/4 tsp. salt
1 1/2 tsp. granulated sugar
3 pkgs. frozen chopped spinach, 10 oz. size
1 cup water
1 onion, chopped
1/3 cup melted unsalted butter
3 tbs. all purpose flour
1 1/2 cups whole milk
1/2 tsp. black pepper

Cut the top off each tomato. Scoop out the pulp but do not damage the tomato shells. Leave about 1/4" shell around the tomato. Sprinkle each tomato with 1/8 teaspoon salt and 1/8 teaspoon granulated sugar. Invert the tomatoes on paper towels and allow them to drain while you prepare the rest of the dish.

In a large sauce pan over medium heat, add the spinach and water. Place a lid on the pan and cook about 8 minutes or until the spinach is tender. Remove the pan from the heat and drain all the liquid from the spinach. Press the spinach with paper towels to remove all moisture.

In a large sauce pan over medium heat, add the onion and butter. Saute for 4 minutes. Sprinkle the all purpose flour over the onion. Stir constantly and cook for 1 minute. Add the spinach, milk, 3/4 teaspoon salt and black pepper. Stir constantly and cook until the sauce thickens and bubbles. Remove the pan from the heat and cool for 5 minutes.

Preheat the oven to 350°. Place the tomatoes in a 9 x 13 casserole dish. Spoon the spinach filling into the tomatoes. Bake for 25 minutes. Remove the dish from the oven and serve.

Creamed Spinach

Makes 4 servings

8 cups fresh spinach, washed and stems removed
1/4 cup unsalted butter
1 onion, chopped
1 garlic clove, minced
1/2 cup sour cream
1/8 tsp. salt
1/4 tsp. black pepper
Pinch of ground nutmeg

In a large skillet over medium heat, add the spinach. Add 1/4 cup water to the spinach. Place a lid on the skillet and cook for 8 minutes or until the spinach is tender. Remove the skillet from the heat and drain all the liquid from the spinach. Press the spinach with paper towels if needed to remove all the moisture.

In a skillet over medium heat, add the butter, onion and garlic. Saute for 5 minutes. Reduce the heat to low. Stir in the spinach, sour cream, salt, black pepper and nutmeg. Cook only until the dish is thoroughly heated. Remove the skillet from the heat and serve.

Stir Fry Spinach

Makes 4 servings

2 tbs. peanut oil
8 cups fresh spinach, washed
1 tsp. salt
1/2 tsp. granulated sugar
2 hard boiled eggs, diced

In a large skillet over medium high heat, add the peanut oil. When the oil is hot, add the half the spinach. Stir constantly until the spinach is coated with the oil. Add the remaining spinach, salt and granulated sugar.

Stir constantly and cook for 4 minutes. Remove the skillet from the heat and sprinkle the hard boiled eggs over the top before serving.

Sauteed Spinach

Makes 3 servings

10 oz. pkg. fresh spinach
2 green onions, chopped
2 tbs. melted unsalted butter
1/4 tsp. granulated sugar
1/4 tsp. salt
1/4 tsp. black pepper
3 lemon wedges

In a large skillet over medium heat, add the spinach, green onions, butter, granulated sugar, salt and black pepper. Saute for 5 minutes or until the spinach is tender. Remove the skillet from the heat. Squeeze the lemon wedges over the top and serve.

Brussels Sprout Stir Fry

Makes 8 servings

6 cups fresh brussels sprouts
1/2 cup unsalted butter
1/3 cup chopped onion
1 small cucumber, peeled and sliced
1 tbs. lemon juice
1 tsp. granulated sugar
1/4 tsp. dried dill
1/2 tsp. salt
1/8 tsp. black pepper
1/4 cup chopped red pimento

Wash the brussels sprouts and remove any tough outer leaves. Pat the brussels sprouts dry with a paper towel. In a large skillet over medium high heat, add the butter and onion. Saute for 4 minutes. Add the brussels sprouts, cucumber, lemon juice, granulated sugar, dill, salt, black pepper and red pimento.

Saute for 5-8 minutes or until the brussels sprouts are tender. Remove the skillet from the heat and serve.

Rosemary Brussels Sprouts & Mushrooms

Makes 4 servings

2 cups fresh brussels sprouts, trimmed
3 tbs. unsalted butter
1 garlic clove, minced
1/2 tsp. crushed dried rosemary
1/2 tsp. grated lemon zest
1/8 tsp. black pepper
1 cup halved fresh button mushrooms

In a sauce pan over medium heat, add the brussels sprouts. Cover with water and bring to a boil. Cook for 6 minutes or until the brussels sprouts are tender. Remove the pan from the heat and drain all the water from the pan.

In a skillet over medium heat, add the butter. When the butter melts, add the garlic, rosemary, lemon zest and black pepper. Stir constantly for 1 minute. Add the mushrooms to the skillet. Saute for 5 minutes. Add the brussels sprouts to the skillet. Saute for 4 minutes. Remove the skillet from the heat and serve.

Lemon & Shallot Brussels Sprouts

Makes 4 servings

2 tbs. olive oil
2 tbs. chopped shallots
1 lb. fresh brussels sprouts, trimmed & quartered
1/2 tsp. salt
1/4 tsp. black pepper
1 tbs. grated lemon zest
2 tbs. fresh lemon juice
2 tbs. unsalted butter

In a large skillet over medium high heat, add the olive oil. When the oil is hot, add the shallots. Saute for 3 minutes. Add the brussels sprouts, salt and black pepper to the skillet. Stir frequently and cook for 8 minutes or until the brussels sprouts begin to brown.

Add the lemon zest, lemon juice and butter to the skillet. Stir constantly and cook until combined and the butter melts. Remove from the heat and serve.

Roasted Brussels Sprouts With Sage Pesto

Makes 6 servings

2 lbs. fresh brussels sprouts, trimmed & halved
1/3 cup plus 1 tbs. olive oil
1/2 cup pistachios
1/3 cup fresh sage leaves
2 tsp. grated lemon zest
2 tbs. fresh lemon juice
1 tsp. salt
1/2 tsp. black pepper

Preheat the oven to 425°. Place the brussels sprouts on a large baking pan. Drizzle 1 tablespoon olive oil over the sprouts. Toss until the sprouts are coated in the oil. Bake for 20 minutes or until the sprouts are lightly browned and tender. Stir occasionally while the brussels sprouts bake.

In a food processor, add the pistachios, sage leaves, lemon zest, lemon juice, salt and black pepper. Process until smooth and combined. With the food processor running, slowly add 1/3 cup olive oil. Process until well combined.

Remove the sprouts from the oven and spoon into a serving bowl. Spoon the pesto over the top. Toss until the sprouts are covered in the pesto. Serve immediately.

Pancetta Brussels Sprouts

Makes 8 servings

2 lbs. fresh brussels sprouts, trimmed
2 tbs. olive oil
1/4 tsp. salt
1/4 tsp. black pepper
6 pancetta slices, 1/8" thick
1 tbs. freshly grated Parmesan cheese

Preheat the oven to 425°. Add the brussels sprouts, olive oil, salt and black pepper to a mixing bowl. Toss until the sprouts are coated in the oil and seasonings. Spread the brussels sprouts on a large baking sheet.

Bake for 20 minutes or until tender and lightly browned. Stir occasionally while the sprouts are baking. Remove the pan from the oven. In a skillet over medium heat, add the pancetta. Cook for 8 minutes or until the pancetta is crisp. Remove the skillet from the heat. Spoon the brussels sprouts into a serving bowl. Sprinkle the pancetta and Parmesan cheese over the top.

Brussels Sprouts in Onion Sauce

Makes 4 servings

3 cups fresh brussels sprouts
2 tbs. plus 2 tsp. unsalted butter
1 cup minced onion
2 tbs. plus 2 tsp. all purpose flour
1 cup whole milk
1 cup half and half
1 1/2 tsp. lemon juice
1/2 tsp. salt
1/4 tsp. dried marjoram

Wash the brussels sprouts and remove any tough outer leaves. Place the brussels sprouts in a large sauce pan over medium heat. Add 1 cup water to the brussels sprouts. Place a lid on the pan and simmer for 10 minutes or until the brussels sprouts are tender. Remove the pan from the heat and drain all the water from the pan. Place the brussels sprouts in a serving dish and keep warm while you make the sauce.

In a sauce pan over medium heat, add the butter. When the butter melts, add the onion. Saute for 5 minutes. Sprinkle the all purpose flour over the onion. Stir constantly for 2 minutes. Add the milk, half and half, lemon juice, salt and marjoram to the pan. Stir constantly and cook until the sauce thickens and bubbles. Remove the sauce from the heat and spoon over the brussels sprouts. Serve hot.

Brussels Sprouts With Water Chestnuts

Makes 8 servings

2 lbs. fresh brussels sprouts, trimmed & halved
2 tbs. unsalted butter
2 tbs. all purpose flour
1/4 tsp. salt
1/4 tsp. black pepper
1 cup chicken broth
8 oz. can sliced water chestnuts, drained

Add the brussels sprouts to a steamer basket. Add 1" of water to a sauce pan over medium heat. Place the basket in the pan. Place a lid on the pan. Cook for 10 minutes or until the sprouts are crisp tender. Remove the pan from the heat.

In a sauce pan over medium heat, add the butter. When the butter melts, add the all purpose flour, salt and black pepper. Stir constantly and cook for 2 minutes. Add the chicken broth to the pan. Stir constantly and cook for 2 minutes or until the sauce thickens and bubbles. Add the water chestnuts to the pan. Stir until combined and remove the pan from the heat. Add the brussels sprouts to a serving bowl. Pour the sauce over the sprouts. Toss until combined and serve.

Orange Brussels Sprouts

Makes 4 servings

4 cups fresh brussels sprouts
1 orange, unpeeled and cut into wedges
1/3 cup fresh orange juice
1 tbs. white wine vinegar
1 tbs. unsalted butter
1 tsp. granulated sugar
1/2 tsp. salt
1/2 tsp. dried dill

Wash the brussels sprouts and remove any tough outer leaves. Add the brussels sprouts, orange wedges, orange juice, white wine vinegar, butter, granulated sugar, salt and dill to a sauce pan over medium heat. Bring to a boil and place a lid on the pan. Reduce the heat to low. Cook for 12 minutes or until the brussels sprouts are tender.

Remove the pan from the heat and serve. You can remove the orange wedges if desired before serving.

Brussels Sprouts with Cashews

Makes 8 servings

3 cups water
2 chicken bouillon cubes
8 cups fresh brussels sprouts, washed
1 1/2 cups sliced carrots
1/3 cup unsalted butter
3/4 cup dry roasted cashew halves
1/4 tsp. dried thyme
1/4 tsp. salt
1/8 tsp. black pepper

In a large sauce pan over medium heat, add the water and chicken bouillon cubes. Bring the water to a boil and add the brussels sprouts and carrots. Bring the vegetables back to a boil and place a lid on the pan. Simmer about 12 minutes or until the vegetables are tender. Remove the pan from the heat and drain all the liquid from the vegetables. Keep the vegetables warm while you prepare the sauce.

Add the butter, cashew halves, thyme, salt and black pepper to a small skillet over medium heat. Stir constantly and cook about 4 minutes or until the cashews are toasted. Remove the skillet from the heat. Place the vegetables on a platter. Pour the cashew sauce over the top and serve.

Sauteed Brussels Sprouts & Cabbage

Makes 4 servings

6 cups thinly sliced green cabbage
2 tbs. olive oil
2 cups fresh brussels sprouts, trimmed & thinly sliced
Salt and black pepper to taste

In a large skillet over medium heat, add the cabbage and olive oil. Saute for 5 minutes. Add the brussels sprouts to the skillet. Saute for 5 minutes. Remove the skillet from the heat and season to taste with salt and black pepper.

Fried Brussels Sprouts

Makes 8 servings

4 cups fresh brussels sprouts
1/2 cup water
1 egg
1 tbs. whole milk
3/4 cup fine dry breadcrumbs
Vegetable oil for frying
Salt and black pepper to taste

Wash the brussels sprouts and remove any tough outer leaves. In a sauce pan over medium heat, add the brussels sprouts and water. Place a lid on the pan and simmer for 7 minutes. Remove the pan from the heat and drain all the water from the brussels sprouts. Shake the sprouts to be sure all the water is removed. Pat them dry with paper towels if needed.

In a small bowl, add the egg and milk. Whisk until well combined. Place the breadcrumbs in a shallow bowl. Dip the brussels sprouts in the egg wash allowing the excess liquid to drip off back into the bowl. Roll the sprouts in the breadcrumbs.

In a deep sauce pan over medium high heat, add vegetable oil to a 3" depth in the pan. The oil temperature needs to be 360°. Drop a few brussels sprouts at a time in the hot oil. Fry for 2 minutes or until golden brown. Remove the brussels sprouts from the oil and drain on paper towels. Repeat until all the sprouts are cooked. Season with salt and black pepper to taste if desired.

Brussels Sprouts in Mustard Sauce

Makes 6 servings

30 fresh brussels sprouts
1 1/2 cups water
1 tbs. unsalted butter
1 tbs. all purpose flour
2/3 cup chicken broth
1/3 cup whole milk
2 tbs. Dijon mustard
1/2 tsp. lemon juice
1/8 tsp. black pepper

Wash the brussels sprouts and remove any tough outer leaves. Cut the stem off the end of the sprouts. Add the brussels sprouts to a sauce pan over medium heat. Add the water and bring to a boil. Place a lid on the pan and reduce the heat to low. Simmer for 15 minutes or until the sprouts are tender. Remove the pan from the heat and drain all the water from the pan.

In a separate sauce pan over low heat, add the butter. When the butter melts, add the all purpose flour. Stir constantly and cook for 1 minute. Add the chicken broth, milk and Dijon mustard. Stir constantly and cook until the sauce thickens and bubbles. Stir in the lemon juice and black pepper. Remove the pan from the heat. Place the brussels sprouts on a serving platter. Pour the sauce over the brussels sprouts and serve.

Southwestern Salsa Kale

Makes 6 servings

1 cup finely chopped fresh tomato
1/2 cup finely chopped yellow bell pepper
2 tbs. finely chopped jalapeno pepper
1 garlic clove, minced
2 tbs. balsamic vinegar
1/4 cup olive oil
2 lbs. fresh kale, washed and stems removed
1 cup finely chopped onion
1/2 cup water
1/4 tsp. salt

In a mixing bowl, add the tomato, yellow bell pepper, jalapeno pepper, garlic, balsamic vinegar and 1 tablespoon olive oil. Stir until combined. Cover the bowl and refrigerate for 1 hour.

Cut the kale into bite size pieces. In a dutch oven over medium heat, add 3 tablespoons olive oil and the onion. Saute for 4 minutes. Add the kale to the pan. Stir constantly until the kale wilts. Add the water to the pan. Place a lid on the pan. Simmer for 10 minutes. Remove the skillet from the heat and stir in the salt. Spoon the kale into a serving bowl.

Remove the tomato salsa from the refrigerator. Spoon the salsa over the top of the kale and serve.

Southern Style Kale

Makes 4 servings

3 slices bacon
2 cups cooked kale
1 tsp. unsalted butter
Salt and black pepper to taste
2 hard boiled eggs, quartered

In a skillet over medium heat, add the bacon. Cook about 5 minutes or until the bacon is crispy. Remove the bacon from the skillet and drain on paper towels. Crumble the bacon into pieces.

Drain off the bacon drippings from the skillet. Add the kale and butter to the skillet. Stir constantly and cook about 2 minutes or until the butter melts and the kale is hot. Remove the skillet from the heat. Season to taste with salt and black pepper.

Spoon the kale into a serving bowl. Sprinkle the bacon over the kale. Place the egg quarters over the top and serve.

Turnip Greens

Makes 6 servings

12 cups fresh turnip greens
5 slices bacon
4 cups water
1 tbs. white vinegar
1 tsp. salt
1/2 tsp. crushed red pepper flakes
1/4 tsp. black pepper

Wash the turnip greens and remove any large stems. Tear the greens into bite size pieces. Add the greens, bacon and water to a dutch oven. Place the pan over medium heat and bring the greens to a boil. Place a lid on the pot and reduce the heat to low. Simmer for 30 minutes.

Add the vinegar, salt, crushed red pepper flakes and black pepper to the pot. Stir until well combined. Simmer for 1 hour. Remove the bacon slices from the greens and discard. Remove the greens from the heat and serve.

Turnip Greens with Turnips

Makes 6 servings

16 cups fresh turnip greens
8 slices bacon
3 turnips, peeled and sliced
1 tsp. granulated sugar
1/4 tsp. salt

Wash the turnips greens thoroughly. Greens tend to be dirty so make sure they are clean. Tear the turnip greens into bite size pieces. In a large dutch oven, add the turnip greens and bacon. Add enough water to cover the greens. Bring the greens to a boil and place a lid on the pan. Reduce the heat to low and simmer for 20 minutes.

Add the turnips, granulated sugar and salt to the pan. Stir until combined and place the lid back on the pan. Simmer about 20 minutes or until the turnips and greens are tender. Remove the bacon slices from the greens and discard. Remove the pan from the heat and serve.

Stir Fried Turnip Greens

Makes 6 servings

22 cups fresh turnips greens or about 2 lbs.
1/2 lb. bacon, chopped
1/2 cup chicken broth
1 tbs. granulated sugar
1 tbs. balsamic vinegar
1/2 tsp. salt
2 apples, cored and cut into thin wedges

Wash the turnip greens and remove any large stems. Stack 3 or 4 greens together and roll tightly. Cut the greens into thin strips. Repeat until all the greens are cut.

In a large skillet over medium heat, add the bacon. Cook about 8 minutes or until the bacon is done and crispy. Remove the bacon from the skillet and drain on paper towels. Leave the bacon drippings in the skillet.

Add the chicken broth, granulated sugar, balsamic vinegar and salt to the bacon drippings. Stir constantly until the sugar melts. Add the greens and increase the heat to medium high. Stir frequently and cook for 10 minutes. Add the apples and bacon to the skillet. Stir constantly and cook for 4 minutes. Remove the skillet from the heat and serve.

Stir Fried Greens

Makes 6 servings

2 tbs. olive oil
6 cups coarsely chopped mixed greens
1 cup shredded red cabbage
1 lime, cut into wedges
Salt and black pepper to taste

Use your favorite greens such as endive, bok choy, collard or mustard greens for the mixed greens if desired.

In a skillet over medium high heat, add the olive oil. When the oil is hot, add the mixed greens and cabbage. Stir constantly and cook for 5 minutes or until the greens are tender. Remove the skillet from the heat.

Serve the greens with the lime wedges and season to taste with salt and black pepper.

Southern Cooked Collards

Makes 6 servings

6 oz. sliced salt pork or bacon
Water
20 cups collard greens, washed and stems removed
Salt and black pepper to taste

In a large dutch oven over medium heat, add the salt pork. Add water to cover the salt pork. Bring the pork to a boil and reduce the heat to low. Cook for 20 minutes.

Add the collard greens to the pan. Stir until the leaves wilt. Do not add water unless needed. The greens will put off a lot of water. Bring the greens to a boil. Place a lid on the pan and simmer for 1 hour. The longer you cook collard greens, the more tender and sweeter they become.

Remove the pan from the heat and season to taste with salt and black pepper. Serve with hot cornbread for a real southern treat.

Collard Greens with Cornmeal Dumpling Patties

Makes 4 servings

16 cups collard greens, washed and stems removed
1 tsp. granulated sugar
1/4 cup bacon drippings
4 oz. ham hock
1 cup plain white or yellow cornmeal
Salt to season

In a large dutch oven over medium heat, add the collard greens. Cover the greens with water and bring the greens to a boil. Add the granulated sugar, bacon drippings and ham hock. Bring the greens back to a boil. Reduce the heat to low and place a lid on the pan. Simmer for 1 hour or until the ham hock and greens are done and tender. Add water if needed to keep the greens covered in water.

In a mixing bowl, add the cornmeal and 1 teaspoon salt. Add broth from the greens to make a moist batter. You will need to form the batter into patties so the batter only needs to be moist. You do not want a runny batter.

Remove the lid from the pan. Bring the greens to a boil. Form the cornmeal batter into small patties. Drop the patties into the greens. Cook for 10-15 minutes or until the patties are cooked and fluffy. Season to taste with salt. Remove the pan from the heat and serve.

You can remove the meat from the ham hock if desired and serve in the greens.

Beer Braised Collard Greens

Makes 6 servings

6 Canadian bacon slices, chopped
1 cup chopped onion
1 tbs. vegetable oil
16 oz. pkg. fresh washed collard greens
12 oz. can light beer
2 tbs. fresh lemon juice
2 tbs. balsamic vinegar
1 tbs. unsalted butter
1 tsp. salt
1/2 tsp. black pepper

In a large dutch oven over medium heat, add the Canadian bacon slices, onion and vegetable oil. Saute for 5 minutes or until the onion is tender. Add the collard greens to the pan. Stir occasionally and cook for 5 minutes or until the collards are wilted.

Add the beer to the pan. Bring the collards to a boil and reduce the heat to low. Place a lid on the pan and simmer for 25 minutes or until the collards are tender. Remove the pan from the heat and stir in the lemon juice, balsamic vinegar, butter, salt and black pepper. Serve hot.

Simple Collard Greens

Makes 3 cups

1 onion, chopped
2 tbs. olive oil
16 oz. pkg. fresh collard greens
1 1/2 tsp. salt
3 cups water

In a dutch oven over medium heat, add the onion and olive oil. Saute for 5 minutes. Wash and chop the collard greens. Add the collard greens, salt and water to the pan. Stir until combined and the collards wilt.

Bring to a boil and place a lid on the pan. Reduce the heat to low and simmer for 30 minutes or until the collard greens are tender. Remove from the heat and serve.

Wine & Bell Pepper Collards

Makes 8 servings

2 pkgs. fresh collard greens, 1 lb. size
1 onion, finely chopped
1 cup dry white wine
1 tbs. granulated sugar
1 tbs. bacon drippings
1 cup water
2 red bell peppers, diced

Remove the stems from the collards. Wash the greens and cut into 1" wide strips. In a dutch oven over medium heat, add the onion, wine, granulated sugar, bacon drippings and water. Stir constantly and cook for 5 minutes.

Add the collard greens and red bell peppers to the pan. Stir until the greens wilt. Bring to a boil and place a lid on the pan. Reduce the heat to low. Simmer for 45 minutes or until the greens are tender. Remove the pan from the heat and serve.

Bourbon Bacon Collards

Makes 10 servings

4 thick bacon slices, diced
3 tbs. unsalted butter
1 1/2 cups diced onion
12 oz. bottle beer
1/2 cup light brown sugar
1/2 cup bourbon
1 tsp. dried crushed red pepper flakes
6 lbs. washed fresh collard greens, trimmed & chopped
1/2 cup apple cider vinegar
1 tsp. salt
1/2 tsp. black pepper

In a dutch oven over medium heat, add the bacon and butter. Saute for 8 minutes or until the bacon is crispy. Remove the bacon from the pan and drain on paper towels. Add the onion to the pan. Saute for 5 minutes. Add the bacon, beer, brown sugar, bourbon and red pepper flakes to the pan. Stir until combined and bring to a boil. Boil for 3 minutes. Add the collards to the pan. Stir until the collards wilt. You will need to add the collards in batches.

Reduce the heat to medium low. Place a lid on the pan. Simmer for 1 hour or until the collards are done to your taste. Add the apple cider vinegar, salt and black pepper to the pan. Stir until combined and remove the pan from the heat.

Braised Endive and Green Peas

Makes 4 servings

4 small heads Belgian endive
2 garlic cloves, halved
2 tbs. melted unsalted butter
1/4 cup chicken broth
1/4 tsp. salt
1/8 tsp. black pepper
10 oz. pkg. frozen green peas, thawed

Lightly rinse the endive with water. Pat the endive dry and trim the ends. Add the endive, garlic and butter to a skillet over medium heat. Stir frequently and cook for 5 minutes. The endive should be lightly browned. Drain all the liquid from the skillet.

Add the chicken broth, salt and black pepper. Place a lid on the skillet and reduce the heat to low. Cook for 4 minutes. Add the green peas and cook for 5 minutes. Remove the skillet from the heat and serve immediately.

Cooked Escarole

Makes 4 servings

1 large head escarole
1 tbs. olive oil
1 garlic clove, minced
Salt and black pepper to taste

Discard the stems from the escarole. Wash the escarole thoroughly and pat dry. Tear the escarole into large pieces. In a skillet over medium heat, add the escarole. Place a lid on the pan and cook for 3 minutes or until the escarole is wilted. Do not add water to the pan. Remove the skillet from the heat.

In a skillet over medium heat, add the olive oil and garlic. Saute the garlic for 2 minutes. Add the escarole and saute for 2 minutes. Season to taste with salt and black pepper. Remove the skillet from the heat and serve.

Skillet Swiss Chard

Makes 4 servings

6 cups Swiss chard leaves
1 tbs. unsalted butter
2 tbs. olive oil
1 garlic clove, minced
Salt and black pepper to taste

You need 6 cups Swiss chard leaves after the stems are removed. This equals about 1 lb. Swiss chard. In a skillet over medium heat, add the butter and olive oil. When the butter melts, add the Swiss chard and garlic. Place a lid on the skillet and cook for 4 minutes.

Remove the lid from the skillet. Stir constantly and cook for 3 minutes. Remove the skillet from the heat. Season to taste with salt and black pepper and serve.

Blue Cheese Coleslaw

Makes 8 servings

6 cups finely shredded cabbage
4 green onions, thinly sliced
1 cup mayonnaise
1/4 cup prepared horseradish
1/2 cup crumbled blue cheese

Add the cabbage and green onions to a serving bowl. Cover the bowl and refrigerate until well chilled.

In a mixing bowl, add the mayonnaise, horseradish and 1/4 cup blue cheese. Stir until well combined. When the cabbage and green onions are chilled, stir in the dressing. Toss until well combined. Sprinkle 1/4 cup blue cheese over the top before serving.

Mexicorn Ranch Slaw

Makes 6 servings

3 cups coleslaw mix
1/4 cup canned Mexicorn, drained
1 jalapeno pepper, seeded and diced
2 tbs. chopped purple onion
1 tbs. minced fresh cilantro
1/2 cup shredded cheddar cheese
1/2 cup prepared ranch salad dressing
1 1/2 tsp. lime juice
1/2 tsp. ground cumin

In a serving bowl, add the coleslaw mix, Mexicorn, jalapeno pepper, onion, cilantro and cheddar cheese. Toss until combined. In a small bowl, add the ranch salad dressing, lime juice and cumin. Stir until combined and pour over the slaw.

Toss until combined. Cover the bowl and refrigerate until chilled.

Chinese Slaw

Makes 8 servings

4 cups chopped Chinese cabbage
11 oz. can mandarin oranges, drained
8 oz. can sliced water chestnuts, drained
1 cup fresh snow peas, trimmed and cut into bite size pieces
1/2 cup chopped red bell pepper
1 green onion, chopped
1/4 cup sesame ginger bottled salad dressing

Add all the ingredients to a serving bowl. Toss until combined and serve.

Texas Corn Slaw

Makes 8 servings

4 cups shredded green cabbage
1 cup shredded red cabbage
1/4 cup chopped purple onion
2 jalapeno peppers, seeded & minced
11 oz. can Mexicorn, drained
1 cup shredded cheddar cheese
3/4 cup prepared ranch dressing
1 tbs. fresh lime juice
1 tsp. ground cumin

In a serving bowl, add the green cabbage, red cabbage, purple onion, jalapeno peppers, Mexicorn and cheddar cheese. Toss until combined. In a small bowl, add the ranch dressing, lime juice and cumin. Whisk until combined and pour over the salad.

Toss until combined. Serve the salad when prepared or chilled.

Sesame Slaw

Makes 4 servings

2 cups shredded green cabbage
1/2 cup shredded purple cabbage
1/3 cup chopped green bell pepper
1 tbs. chopped onion
1/4 cup cider vinegar
3 tbs. granulated sugar
1 tsp. toasted sesame seeds
1/4 tsp. salt

Add the green cabbage, purple cabbage, green bell pepper and onion to a serving bowl. In a small bowl, add the cider vinegar, granulated sugar, sesame seeds and salt. Stir until combined and pour over the cabbage. Toss until well combined.

Cover the bowl and refrigerate until chilled.

Old Fashioned Coleslaw

Makes 12 servings

10 cups shredded cabbage
2 cups shredded carrots
1/4 cup chopped sweet pickle
1/2 cup mayonnaise
1/2 tsp. salt
1/2 tsp. granulated sugar
1/2 tsp. dry mustard
1/2 tsp. black pepper

Add the cabbage and carrots to a large bowl. In a mixing bowl, add the sweet pickle, mayonnaise, salt, granulated sugar, dry mustard and black pepper. Stir until combined.

Add the dressing to the cabbage and carrots. Toss until well combined. Cover the bowl and chill for 2 hours before serving.

Coleslaw with Tomatoes

Makes 8 servings

8 cups shredded cabbage
1 green bell pepper, cut into rings
2 onions, sliced and separated into rings
1/2 cup plus 2 tsp. granulated sugar
1 cup vinegar
1 tsp. celery seeds
3/4 cup vegetable oil
1 tsp. dry mustard
2 tsp. salt
1 cup cherry tomatoes, halved

In a large bowl, add the cabbage. Place the green bell pepper rings over the cabbage. Place the onion rings over the green bell pepper. Sprinkle the vegetables with 1/2 cup granulated sugar.

In a sauce pan over medium heat, add the vinegar, celery seeds, 2 teaspoon granulated sugar, vegetable oil, dry mustard and salt. Stir constantly and bring the dressing to a boil. Remove the pan from the heat and pour the dressing over the vegetables in the bowl. Cover the bowl and chill for 4 hours.

Add the tomatoes and toss until well combined.

Chili Coleslaw

Makes 8 servings

1/2 cup mayonnaise
1/4 cup chili sauce
1/2 tsp. salt
5 cups finely shredded cabbage
1 cup thinly sliced celery
2 tbs. grated onion
6 oz. jar sliced red pimentos, drained

In a small bowl, add the mayonnaise, chili sauce and salt. Stir until combined. Add the cabbage, celery, onion and red pimentos to a large bowl. Toss until combined.

Add the mayonnaise dressing and toss until combined. Cover the bowl and chill for 2 hours before serving.

Lemon Butter Cabbage

Makes 6 servings

1 1/2 tbs. unsalted butter
1 1/2 tbs. vegetable oil
1 tsp. caraway seeds
1 head cabbage, chopped
1 tsp. grated lemon zest
2 tbs. lemon juice
1/4 tsp. salt
1/8 tsp. black pepper

In a skillet over medium high heat, add the butter, vegetable oil and caraway seeds. Stir constantly and cook for 2 minutes. Add the cabbage and cook for 4 minutes. Place a lid on the pan and reduce the heat to medium. Cook for 2 minutes.

Add the lemon zest, lemon juice, salt and black pepper to the skillet. Stir constantly and cook for 2 minutes. Remove the skillet from the heat and serve.

Orange Cranberry Cabbage

Makes 6 servings

10 cups shredded cabbage
3 tbs. olive oil
6 oz. pkg. sweetened dried cranberries
1 tsp. grated orange zest
3/4 cup orange juice
1/2 cup rice wine vinegar
1 tbs. honey
1 tsp. salt
1/2 tsp. black pepper
1/2 tsp. grated nutmeg
3 tbs. unsalted butter

In a dutch oven over medium heat, add the cabbage and olive oil. Saute for 5 minutes or until the cabbage is tender. Add the cranberries, orange zest, orange juice, rice wine vinegar, honey, salt, black pepper and nutmeg to the pan. Stir until well combined. Saute for 6 minutes or until the the liquid reduces.

Remove the pan from the heat and add the butter. Stir until the butter melts and serve.

Cabbage Saute

Makes 8 servings

2 tbs. unsalted butter
4 cups chopped cabbage
1/2 cup sliced onion
2 cups chopped fresh tomatoes
1 apple, cored and chopped
1 tsp. salt
1 tsp. dried dill
1/4 tsp. black pepper

In a large skillet over medium heat, add the butter. When the butter melts, add the cabbage and onion. Saute for 5 minutes. Add the tomatoes, apple, salt, dill and black pepper to the skillet. Stir until combined.

Place a lid on the skillet. Cook for 5 minutes. Remove the skillet from the heat and serve.

Stir Fry Cabbage

Makes 4 servings

2 tbs. vegetable oil
1 tsp. sesame oil
1 garlic clove, minced
1 tsp. grated fresh ginger
1 cup shredded green cabbage
1 cup shredded Napa cabbage
1 cup shredded bok choy
1/2 cup chopped green onions
1 tbs. soy sauce
2 tsp. toasted sesame seeds, optional

In a large skillet over medium high heat, add the vegetable oil, sesame oil, garlic and ginger. When the oils are hot, add the green cabbage, Napa cabbage, bok choy, green onions and soy sauce.

Stir constantly and cook for 3 minutes. Remove the skillet from the heat and sprinkle the sesame seeds over the top.

Cabbage and Dumplings

Makes 8 servings

1 medium head cabbage
3/4 cup water
3/4 cup vinegar
3/4 cup bacon drippings
1 tbs. caraway seed
3 cups Bisquick
2 eggs
Milk as needed

Shred the cabbage and add to a large sauce pan. Add the water, vinegar, bacon drippings and caraway seed to the sauce pan. Place the pan over medium heat and bring the cabbage to a boil. Place a lid on the pan and cook for 30 minutes. Stir occasionally while the cabbage cooks.

In a mixing bowl, add the Bisquick and eggs. Stir until well blended. You only need to add milk if needed to moisten the dough. The dough needs to be moist enough to form into small balls but the dough should not be wet. Form the dough into small balls.

Remove the lid from the cabbage. The cabbage needs to be at a boiling simmer. Drop the dumplings into the sauce pan. Place the lid on the pan and cook for 15-20 minutes or until the dumplings are cooked and fluffy. Remove the pan from the heat and serve.

Smothered Cabbage Wedges

Makes 8 servings

1 large head cabbage
1/2 cup finely chopped green bell pepper
1/4 cup finely chopped onion
1/4 cup melted unsalted butter
1/4 cup all purpose flour
2 cups whole milk
1/2 tsp. salt
1/8 tsp. black pepper
1/2 cup mayonnaise
3/4 cup shredded cheddar cheese
3 tbs. chili sauce

Core the cabbage and cut into 8 wedges. Place the cabbage wedges in a large sauce pan over medium heat. Add 2 cups water to the pan and place a lid on the pan. Cook for 10 minutes. Remove the pan from the heat and drain all the water from the cabbage. Place the cabbage wedges in a 9 x 13 casserole dish.

In a skillet over medium heat, add the green bell pepper, onion and butter. Saute for 5 minutes. Sprinkle the all purpose flour over the vegetables. Stir constantly and cook for 1 minute. Add the milk, salt and black pepper to the skillet. Stir constantly and cook until the sauce thickens and bubbles. Remove the skillet from the heat and pour the sauce over the cabbage wedges.

Preheat the oven to 350°. Bake for 20 minutes. In a small bowl, stir together the mayonnaise, cheddar cheese and chili sauce. Stir until combined and spoon over the cabbage. Bake for 5 minutes. Remove the dish from the oven and serve.

Cabbage Stroganoff

Makes 6 servings

1 large head cabbage
1/4 cup water
1 tsp. salt
2 tbs. unsalted butter, softened
1 tbs. granulated sugar
1 tbs. vinegar
1 cup sour cream

Shred the cabbage and place in a large dutch oven. Add the water and salt to the pan. Place the pan over medium heat and bring the cabbage to a boil. Place a lid on the pan and boil for 5 minutes. Remove the pan from the heat and drain all liquid from the pan.

Preheat the oven to 350°. Spray a 1 1/2 quart casserole dish with non stick cooking spray. Spoon the cabbage into the casserole dish. In a mixing bowl, add the butter, granulated sugar, vinegar and sour cream. Stir until combined and spoon over the cabbage. Toss until the cabbage is coated in the sauce. Bake for 20 minutes or until the dish is thoroughly heated. Remove from the oven and serve.

Cheese Scalloped Cabbage

Makes 8 servings

1 large cabbage
1/2 cup unsalted butter
1/4 cup all purpose flour
2 cups whole milk
1/2 tsp. salt
1/4 tsp. black pepper
Pinch of ground nutmeg
2 cups shredded cheddar cheese
1 cup soft breadcrumbs

Core the cabbage and cut into 8 wedges. Place the cabbage wedges in a large sauce pan over medium heat. Add 2 cups water to the pan and place a lid on the pan. Cook for 10 minutes. Remove the pan from the heat and drain all the water from the cabbage.

In a sauce pan over medium heat, add the butter. When the butter melts, add the all purpose flour. Stir constantly and cook for 1 minute. Add the milk, salt, black pepper and nutmeg to the pan. Stir constantly and cook until the sauce thickens and bubbles. Remove the pan from the heat and add the cheddar cheese. Stir until the cheese melts. Preheat the oven to 350°. Place half the cabbage in a 3 quart casserole dish. Pour half the cheese sauce over the cabbage. Repeat the layering process one more time. Sprinkle the breadcrumbs over the top. Bake for 30 minutes. Remove the dish from the oven and serve.

Cabbage Vegetable Skillet

Makes 6 servings

1 tbs. vegetable oil
3 cups shredded cabbage
1/4 eggplant, peeled and cut into thin strips
1 onion, thinly sliced
1 cup cooked bean sprouts
1 green bell pepper, cut into thin strips
2 tomatoes, diced
1/2 cup thinly sliced carrots
1 tsp. salt
1/2 tsp. black pepper

Add the vegetable oil to a large skillet over medium heat. When the oil is hot, add all the ingredients to the skillet. Stir frequently and cook about 10 minutes or until the vegetables are tender. Remove the skillet from the heat and serve.

Bubbling Cabbage

Makes 6 servings

1 savoy cabbage, chopped
1 cup Sprite
5 anise seeds, crushed
1/8 tsp. salt
1/8 tsp. black pepper
3 tbs. unsalted butter

Add the cabbage, Sprite, anise seeds, salt and black pepper to a sauce pan. Place the pan over medium heat and bring to a boil. Place a lid on the pan and reduce the heat to low. Simmer for 8 minutes or until the cabbage is tender.

Add the butter and toss until the butter melts. Remove the pan from the heat and serve.

Wilted Cabbage

Makes 6 servings

4 slices bacon
1/2 cup chopped green bell pepper
2 tbs. vinegar
2 tbs. water
1 tbs. granulated sugar
1/2 tsp. salt
4 cups shredded cabbage
1 1/2 cups finely chopped apple, peeled

In a large skillet over medium heat, add the bacon. Cook about 6 minutes or until the bacon is done and crisp. Remove the bacon from the skillet and drain on paper towels. Leave the bacon drippings in the skillet.

Add the green bell pepper to the skillet. Saute for 4 minutes. Add the vinegar, water, granulated sugar and salt to the skillet. Stir until combined. Bring to a boil and add the cabbage and apple. Stir until combined. Place a lid on the skillet and cook about 6 minutes or until the cabbage is tender.

Remove the skillet from the heat and stir in the bacon.

Country Style Cabbage

Makes 6 servings

3 tbs. unsalted butter
2 onions, diced
1 green bell pepper, cut into thin strips
1 medium cabbage, cut into 6 wedges
2 large tomatoes, cut into wedges
3/4 tsp. salt
1/4 tsp. black pepper

In a large skillet over low heat, add the butter and onion. Saute for 4 minutes. Add the green bell pepper to the skillet. Place a lid on the skillet and simmer for 5 minutes.

Arrange the cabbage and tomatoes over the skillet. Sprinkle the salt and black pepper over the cabbage and tomatoes. Place the lid back on the pan and simmer for 20 minutes or until the cabbage is tender. Remove the skillet from the heat and serve.

German Red Cabbage

Makes 6 servings

1 head red cabbage
1/2 cup onion, chopped
2 tbs. granulated sugar
1 tsp. salt
1 bay leaf
1/4 cup water
2 tbs. red wine vinegar
1 apple, peeled and chopped
3 slices bacon, cooked and crumbled

Core the cabbage and cut the cabbage into 6 wedges. Place the cabbage wedges in a large sauce pan over medium heat. Add the onion, granulated sugar, salt, bay leaf and water. Bring the cabbage to a boil and place a lid on the pan. Reduce the heat to low and simmer for 15 minutes.

Add the red wine vinegar and the apple to the pan. Simmer for 5 minutes or until the cabbage is tender. Remove the cabbage wedges from the pan using a slotted spoon and place on a serving platter. Using a slotted spoon, remove the onion and apple from the pan. Spoon the onion and apple over the cabbage wedges. Sprinkle the bacon over the top before serving.

Artichoke Hearts with Lemon

Makes 4 servings

1/3 cup minced onion
1 garlic clove, crushed
1 tbs. melted unsalted butter
2 cans drained & halved artichoke hearts, 14 oz. size
1 cup chicken broth
3 tbs. lemon juice
1 tsp. dried oregano
1 tsp. salt

In a sauce pan over medium heat, add the onion, garlic and butter. Saute for 5 minutes. Add the artichokes, chicken broth, lemon juice, oregano and salt to the pan. Simmer for 10 minutes. Remove from the heat and serve.

Garlic Green Beans

This simple dish is my most requested recipe for barbecue's, potlucks and holidays!

Makes 12 servings

3 lbs. fresh green beans, trimmed
1 1/2 tsp. salt
3 large garlic cloves, thinly sliced
2 tbs. olive oil
1/2 tsp. black pepper

Add the green beans and 1/2 teaspoon salt to a large sauce pan over medium heat. Cover the green beans with water. Bring to a boil and place a lid on the pan. Cook for 5 minutes or until the green beans are crisp tender. Remove the pan from the heat.

In a skillet over medium heat, add half the garlic and 1 tablespoon olive oil. Saute for 1 minute. Add half the green beans to the skillet. Sprinkle 1/2 teaspoon salt and 1/4 teaspoon black pepper over the green beans. Saute for 3 minutes. Spoon the green beans into a serving dish. Repeat this step using the remaining olive oil, garlic, salt, black pepper and green beans.

Do not try to cook all the green beans and garlic at one time. The taste is not the same and the garlic usually ends up tasting bitter.

Basil Green Beans

Makes 3 servings

2 cups frozen French style green beans
2 tsp. unsalted butter
1/2 tsp. dried basil
1/2 tsp. lemon pepper seasoning
Salt to taste

Add the green beans, butter, basil and lemon pepper seasoning to a sauce pan over medium heat. Stir until combined and bring to a boil. Reduce the heat to low and place a lid on the pan. Simmer for 6 minutes or until the green beans are tender.

Remove the pan from the heat and season to taste with salt.

Green Beans & New Potatoes

Makes 12 servings

3 1/2 cups small red new potatoes, quartered
16 oz. pkg. frozen cut green beans, thawed & drained
1/3 cup olive oil
1/4 cup cider vinegar
1 tsp. granulated sugar
1 tsp. dried tarragon
1/2 tsp. salt
1/8 tsp. black pepper

In a sauce pan over medium heat, add the potatoes. Cover the potatoes with water and bring to a boil. Reduce the heat to low. Cook for 12 minutes or until the potatoes are tender. Add the green beans to the pan. Cook for 5 minutes or until the green beans are crisp tender. Remove the pan from the heat and drain the liquid from the pan.

In a jar with a lid, add the olive oil, cider vinegar, granulated sugar, tarragon, salt and black pepper. Place the lid on the jar and shake until combined. Pour the dressing over the potatoes and green beans. Toss until combined and serve.

Green Bean Saute

Makes 8 servings

1 lb. fresh green beans, trimmed
1 cup frozen pearl onions
2 tbs. unsalted butter
1 red bell pepper, cut into 1/4" wide strips
1 tsp. chopped fresh thyme
1/8 tsp. salt

Cut the green beans in half crosswise and add to a large skillet over medium heat. Cover the green beans with water and bring to a boil. Cook for 5 minutes. Remove from the heat and drain all the water from the green beans.

Place the skillet back on the stove. Add the onions, butter, red bell pepper, thyme and salt. Stir constantly and cook for 6 minutes or until the vegetables are tender. Remove from the heat and serve.

Creole Green Beans

Makes 6 servings

4 cups cut fresh green beans
5 bacon slices, diced
1 cup chopped onion
1/2 cup chopped green bell pepper
2 tbs. all purpose flour
2 tbs. light brown sugar
1 tbs. Worcestershire sauce
1 tsp. salt
1/2 tsp. black pepper
1/2 tsp. dry mustard
14 oz. can diced tomatoes

In a sauce pan over medium heat, add the green beans. Cover the beans with water and bring to a boil. Cook for 8 minutes or until the green beans are crisp tender. Remove the pan from the heat and drain all the water from the pan.

While the green beans are cooking, make the rest of the dish. In a skillet over medium heat, add the bacon, onion and green bell pepper. Saute for 8 minutes or until the bacon is crisp. Remove the bacon and vegetables from the skillet using a slotted spoon and drain on paper towels.

Add the all purpose flour, brown sugar, Worcestershire sauce, salt, black pepper and mustard to the skillet. Stir until well combined. Add the tomatoes with juice to the skillet. Stir constantly and bring to a boil. Cook for 2 minutes or until the sauce thickens. Add the green beans, bacon and vegetables back to the skillet. Stir until combined and thoroughly heated. Remove the skillet from the heat and serve.

Roasted Green Beans With Sun Dried Tomatoes

Makes 8 servings

1 1/2 lbs. fresh green beans, trimmed
1/2 cup sun dried tomatoes in oil, chopped
1/3 cup chopped walnuts
3 tbs. melted unsalted butter
3 tbs. olive oil
1 tsp. salt
1/2 tsp. black pepper

Preheat the oven to 425°. Add all the ingredients to a mixing bowl. Toss until combined. Spread the green beans onto a baking sheet. Bake for 15 minutes or until the green beans are tender. Remove from the oven and serve.

Herb Green Beans

Makes 8 servings

8 cups fresh green beans
1 onion, sliced
1 garlic clove, minced
1 tbs. olive oil
3/4 cup water
1/2 tsp. granulated sugar
1/2 tsp. salt
1/2 tsp. black pepper
1/4 tsp. dried tarragon

Wash and trim the ends from the green beans. You can leave the green beans whole or cut into pieces. In a dutch oven over medium heat, add the onion, garlic and olive oil. Saute for 4 minutes. Add the green beans, water, granulated sugar, salt, black pepper and tarragon to the pan.

Bring the green beans to a boil and place a lid on the pan. Reduce the heat to low. Simmer for 20 minutes or until the green beans are tender. Remove the pan from the heat and serve.

Barbecue Green Beans

Makes 6 servings

5 slices bacon
3/4 cup chopped onion
2 cans drained cut green beans, 15 oz. size
1/2 cup barbecue sauce
3 tbs. ketchup
1 garlic clove, minced
1/8 tsp. black pepper

In a large skillet over medium heat, add the bacon. Cook about 7 minutes or until the bacon is cooked and crisp. Remove the bacon from the skillet and drain on paper towels. Leave the bacon drippings in the skillet. Crumble the bacon into pieces.

Add the onion to the skillet. Saute for 4 minutes. Add the bacon, green beans, barbecue sauce, ketchup, garlic and black pepper to the skillet. Stir constantly and cook for 5 minutes. Remove the skillet from the heat and serve.

Blue Cheese Green Beans

Makes 4 servings

1/2 cup water
1/4 tsp. salt
9 oz. pkg. frozen French cut green beans
1 1/2 tbs. unsalted butter
2 tbs. crumbled blue cheese
1/8 tsp. black pepper
1/2 cup soft breadcrumbs

In a sauce pan over medium heat, add the water, salt and green beans. Bring the beans to a boil and cook for 8 minutes or until the green beans are crisp tender. Remove the pan from the heat and drain all the water from the pan. Add 1 tablespoon butter, blue cheese and black pepper to the green beans. Toss until combined.

Spray a 1 quart casserole dish with non stick cooking spray. Preheat the oven to 350°. Spoon the green beans into the casserole dish. In a small sauce pan over medium heat, add 1/2 tablespoon butter and the breadcrumbs. Stir constantly and cook until the breadcrumbs are toasted. Remove the pan from the heat and sprinkle the breadcrumbs over the top of the green beans.

Bake for 15 minutes or until the dish is hot and bubbly. Remove from the oven and serve.

Blue Cheese Bacon Green Beans

Makes 6 servings

6 bacon slices, diced
1 lb. fresh green beans, trimmed & cut into 2" pieces
1/2 cup crumbled blue cheese
1/3 cup chopped pecans
Black pepper to taste

In a skillet over medium heat, add the bacon. Cook for 8 minutes or until the bacon is crispy. Remove the bacon from the skillet and drain on paper towels.

Add the green beans to the skillet. Saute for 8 minutes or until the green beans are crisp tender. Add the bacon, blue cheese and pecans to the skillet. Saute for 2 minutes. Remove the skillet from the heat and season to taste with black pepper.

Green Beans with Buttered Pecans

Makes 4 servings

4 cups fresh green beans, washed and ends trimmed
4 cups water
2 tbs. unsalted butter
4 tbs. chopped pecans
1/4 tsp. black pepper
1/2 tsp. salt

In a sauce pan over medium heat, add the green beans and water. Bring the green beans to a boil and cook for 10 minutes or until crisp tender. Remove the pan from the heat and drain all the water from the pan.

In a skillet over medium heat, add the butter, pecans, black pepper and salt. Stir constantly and cook for 3 minutes or until the pecans are golden brown. Add the green beans and toss until the green beans are coated with the butter. Cook for 2 minutes. Remove the skillet from the heat and serve.

Green Beans with Pepper Strips

Makes 4 servings

5 cups fresh green beans
2 tbs. olive oil
2 green onions, diced
1 garlic clove, minced
1 red bell pepper, cut into thin strips
1 tsp. dried marjoram
2 tbs. water
1/4 tsp. salt
1/8 tsp. black pepper
1/8 tsp. cayenne pepper

Trim the ends from the green beans and cut into bite size pieces. In a large skillet over medium heat, add the olive oil. When the oil is hot, add the green onions. Stir constantly and cook for 1 minute. Add the green beans, garlic, red bell pepper, marjoram, water, salt, black pepper and cayenne pepper to the skillet.

Stir constantly and cook for 2 minutes. Bring the green beans to a boil and place a lid on the pan. Reduce the heat to low and cook about 20 minutes or until the green beans are tender. Remove the skillet from the heat and serve.

Cheesy Green Beans

Makes 4 servings

4 cups fresh green beans, trimmed and washed
1 cup water
1 envelope dry onion soup mix
3 tbs. melted unsalted butter
1/3 cup toasted slivered almonds
3 tbs. freshly grated Parmesan cheese
1/2 tsp. paprika

Cut the green beans into 2" pieces. Add the green beans, water and onion soup mix to a sauce pan over medium heat. Bring the green beans to a boil and place a lid on the pan. Reduce the heat to low and simmer for 15 minutes.

Drain all the water from the pan. Add the butter, almonds and Parmesan cheese to the pan. Toss until well combined and the Parmesan cheese and butter melt. Remove the pan from the heat and sprinkle the paprika over the top before serving.

Spanish Green Beans

Makes 6 servings

4 cups fresh green beans, trimmed and washed
1 onion, chopped
1 garlic clove, minced
2 tbs. unsalted melted butter
1 1/2 tsp. salt
1/4 tsp. black pepper
5 tomatoes, diced
2 green bell peppers, chopped

Cut the green beans into 1 1/2" pieces. In a large skillet over medium heat, add the onion, garlic and melted butter. Saute for 4 minutes. Add the green beans, salt and black pepper. Stir frequently and cook about 5 minutes or until the green beans are crisp tender.

Stir in the tomatoes and green bell peppers. Reduce the heat to low and place a lid on the skillet. Simmer for 30 minutes. Remove the skillet from the heat and serve.

French Quarter Green Beans

Makes 8 servings

3 pkgs. frozen cut green beans, 10 oz. size
3 tbs. unsalted butter
10.75 oz. can cream of mushroom soup
3 oz. pkg. cream cheese, cubed
1 tsp. dried minced onion
8 oz. can sliced water chestnuts, drained
1/4 tsp. garlic salt
1/4 tsp. black pepper
1/4 cup toasted slivered almonds

In a large sauce pan over medium heat, add the green beans. Cover the green beans with water. Bring to a boil and place a lid on the pan. Reduce the heat to low and simmer for 15 minutes or until the green beans are tender. Remove the pan from the heat and drain all the water from the green beans.

In a small sauce pan over medium heat, add the butter. When the butter melts, add the cream of mushroom soup, cream cheese and minced onion. Stir constantly until combined and the cream cheese melts. Stir in the water chestnuts, garlic salt and black pepper. Remove the pan from the heat and add to the green beans. Preheat the oven to 375°. Spoon the green beans into a 2 quart casserole dish. Sprinkle the almonds over the top of the dish. Bake for 45 minutes. Remove the dish from the oven and serve.

Lemon Green Beans

Makes 4 servings

4 cups fresh green beans
4 tbs. minced onion
4 tbs. melted unsalted butter
2 tbs. fresh lemon juice
1/2 tsp. salt
1/4 tsp. black pepper

Wash and trim the ends from the green beans. Cut the green beans into 1 1/2" pieces. Add the green beans and 1 cup water to a sauce pan over medium heat. Place a lid on the pan and simmer for 20 minutes or until the green beans are tender. Remove the pan from the heat and drain all the water from the green beans. Keep the green beans warm while you prepare the sauce.

In a small sauce pan over medium heat, add the onion and butter. Saute for 5 minutes. Add the lemon juice, salt and black pepper. Stir constantly and cook for 3 minutes. Remove the pan from the heat. Place the green beans in a serving dish. Spoon the sauce over the green beans. Toss until combined and serve.

Lemon Dill Green Beans

Makes 6 servings

1 lb. fresh green beans, trimmed
2 tbs. lemon juice
2 tbs. olive oil
2 tbs. minced fresh dill
1/4 tsp. salt

Add the green beans to a steamer basket. Add 1" water to a sauce pan over medium heat. Bring the water to a boil and add the steamer basket. Place a lid on the pan and steam for 8 minutes or until the green beans are crisp tender. Remove the pan from the heat.

In a jar with a lid, add the lemon juice, olive oil, dill and salt. Place the lid on the jar and shake until well combined. Add the green beans to a serving bowl. Pour the dressing over the green beans. Toss until combined and serve.

Holiday Green Beans

Makes 8 servings

10 cups fresh green beans
3 cups water
1 cup sliced fresh mushrooms
1/3 cup chopped onion
3 garlic cloves, minced
8 oz. can sliced water chestnuts, drained
1/2 tsp. salt
1/2 tsp. black pepper
1/2 tsp. dried basil
1 tsp. dried Italian seasoning
1/3 cup olive oil
1/4 cup grated Parmesan cheese

Wash the green beans and trim the ends. Add the green beans and water to a dutch oven over medium heat. Bring the green beans to a boil and place a lid on the pan. Reduce the heat to low and simmer about 8 minutes or until the green beans are crisp tender. Remove the green beans from the heat and drain all the water from the pan. Rinse the green beans in cold water until they are chilled.

In a large skillet over medium heat, add the mushrooms, onion, garlic, water chestnuts, salt, black pepper, basil, Italian seasoning and olive oil. Saute the vegetables for 5 minutes. Add the green beans to the skillet. Stir constantly and cook for 5 minutes. Remove the skillet from the heat and sprinkle the Parmesan cheese over the top before serving.

Zucchini Green Beans

Makes 6 servings

4 cups fresh green beans, washed and ends trimmed
1/2 cup minced onion
1/4 cup unsalted butter
2 zucchini, thinly sliced
4 bacon slices, cooked and crumbled
3/4 tsp. salt
1/8 tsp. black pepper

Cut the green beans into 1 1/2" pieces. Add the green beans to a sauce pan over medium heat. Cover the green beans with water and bring to a boil. Place a lid on the pan and reduce the heat to low. Simmer for 20 minutes. Remove the pan from the heat and drain all the water from the green beans.

In a large skillet over medium heat, add the onion, butter and zucchini. Saute for 5 minutes. Add the green beans, bacon, salt and black pepper to the skillet. Stir constantly and cook for 4 minutes. Remove the skillet from the heat and serve.

Butter Garlic Green Beans

Makes 4 servings

4 cups fresh green beans, washed and ends trimmed
2 cups water
4 garlic cloves, minced
3 tbs. unsalted butter
1/8 tsp. salt
1/8 tsp. black pepper
1/3 cup chopped fresh parsley

Add the green beans and water to a sauce pan over medium heat. Bring the green beans to a boil. Place a lid on the pan and reduce the heat to low. Simmer for 20 minutes. Remove the pan from the heat and drain all the water from the green beans.

In a large skillet over medium heat, add the garlic and butter. Stir constantly and cook for 3 minutes. Add the salt, black pepper and parsley. Cook for 1 minute. Add the green beans to the skillet. Stir constantly and cook for 2 minutes. Remove the skillet from the heat and serve.

Grilled Asparagus & New Potatoes

Makes 4 servings

2 tbs. olive oil
1/2 tsp. salt
1/2 tsp. lemon pepper seasoning
6 small new potatoes, quartered
1 lb. fresh asparagus spears, trimmed

Have your grill hot and ready. Cut four 18" x 12" pieces aluminum foil. In a small bowl, add the olive oil, salt and lemon pepper. Stir until combined. Divide the new potatoes and asparagus among the four pieces aluminum foil. Place the vegetables in the center of the foil. Drizzle the olive oil over the vegetables. Lightly toss until the vegetables are coated in the oil. Fold the foil to form a packet.

Place the packets on the grill. Cook for 20 minutes or until the vegetables are tender. Remove from the grill and serve. Be careful when opening the packets as hot steam will escape.

Asparagus in Squash Rings

Makes 12 servings

12 cups fresh asparagus spears
6 1/2 cups water
5 small yellow squash, cut into 1/2" slices
1/2 cup unsalted butter
1/4 cup lemon juice
1 tsp. fines herbs

Cut off the tough woody ends from the asparagus. Trim off the rough scales on the asparagus. In a large sauce pan over medium heat, add the asparagus and 6 cups water. Bring the asparagus to a boil. Place a lid on the pan and reduce the heat to low. Simmer for 8 minutes or until the asparagus is crisp tender. Remove the pan from the heat and drain all the water from the pan.

In a separate sauce pan over medium heat, add the squash and 1/2 cup water. Place a lid on the pan and bring the squash to a boil. Boil for 3 minutes. Remove the pan from the heat and drain all the water from the pan. Rinse the squash with cold water and drain all the water again.

Remove the centers from the squash slices with a spoon. Place 3 or 4 asparagus spears inside the center of the squash slices. Place the asparagus on a serving platter and keep warm.

In the sauce pan used to cook the squash, add the butter, lemon juice and fines herbs. Place the pan over low heat and cook until the butter melts. Stir constantly and cook for 30 seconds. Remove the pan from the heat and pour over the asparagus.

Roasted Orange Ginger Asparagus

Makes 6 servings

2 lbs. fresh asparagus, trimmed
1/4 cup orange juice
2 tbs. olive oil
1 tbs. grated fresh ginger
1 tbs. Dijon mustard
1/2 tsp. salt
1/4 tsp. black pepper
1 tsp. grated orange zest

Preheat the oven to 400°. Spray a large baking sheet with non stick cooking spray. Place the asparagus on the baking sheet. In a small bowl, add the orange juice, olive oil, ginger, Dijon mustard, salt and black pepper. Whisk until combined and drizzle over the asparagus.

Toss until the asparagus is coated in the dressing. Bake for 15 minutes or until the asparagus is done to your taste. Remove the pan from the oven and sprinkle the orange zest over the top.

Asparagus Mushroom Saute

Makes 4 servings

3 cups fresh asparagus spears
1/4 cup chopped green onions
2 tbs. olive oil
2 cups sliced fresh mushrooms
1 tsp. dried thyme
1/2 tsp. salt
1/4 tsp. black pepper
3 tbs. dry white wine
1/3 cup freshly grated Parmesan cheese
1 tsp. grated lemon zest

Trim the tough woody ends and the outer scales from the asparagus. Cut the asparagus into 1" pieces. In a large skillet, add the green onions and olive oil. Saute for 3 minutes. Add the asparagus, mushrooms, thyme, salt and black pepper. Saute the vegetables for 5 minutes.

Add the white wine and cook for 3 minutes. Sprinkle the Parmesan cheese and lemon zest over the top. Remove the skillet from the heat and serve.

Jeweled Asparagus

Makes 10 servings

1/2 cup unsalted butter
1 green bell pepper, thinly sliced
1 cup sliced celery
2 tbs. lemon juice
2 oz. jar diced red pimentos, drained
8 oz. can sliced water chestnuts
2 lbs. cooked fresh asparagus

In a large skillet over medium heat, add the butter. When the butter melts, add the green bell pepper and celery. Saute for 5 minutes. Add the lemon juice, red pimentos and water chestnuts. Stir frequently and cook for 5 minutes.

Place the cooked fresh asparagus on a serving platter. Remove the skillet from the heat and pour the sauce over the asparagus.

Marinated Asparagus

Makes 4 servings

15 oz. can asparagus spears, drained
1/4 cup vegetable oil
1 tbs. dried parsley flakes
3 tbs. vinegar
2 tbs chopped red pimento
3/4 tsp. salt
1/4 tsp. black pepper

Place the asparagus in a shallow dish. In a small bowl, add the vegetable oil, parsley, vinegar, red pimento, salt and black pepper. Whisk until combined. Pour the dressing over the asparagus.

Cover the dish and chill for 4 hours before serving.

Sweet and Sour Asparagus

Makes 8 servings

4 cups fresh asparagus spears, cleaned and trimmed
1 cup water
2/3 cup white vinegar
1/2 cup granulated sugar
1/2 tsp. salt
1 tsp. whole cloves
3 sticks cinnamon, about 3" each
1 1/2 tsp. celery seeds

In a large sauce pan over medium heat, add the asparagus. Add 1/2 cup water to the pan and place a lid on the pan. Simmer about 8 minutes or until the asparagus is crisp tender. Remove the pan from the heat and drain all the water from the pan.

Place the asparagus in a 9 x 13 casserole dish. In the sauce pan used to cook the asparagus, add the white vinegar, granulated sugar, 1/2 cup water, salt, cloves, cinnamon and celery seeds. Bring the sauce to a boil and remove the pan from the heat. Stir until the granulated sugar is dissolved. Pour the sauce over the asparagus. Cover the dish and refrigerate for 24 hours.

Remove the dish from the refrigerator and drain off all the liquid. Remove and discard the cloves and cinnamon sticks. Place the asparagus on a plate and serve.

Asparagus Supreme

Makes 12 servings

8 cups fresh asparagus spears
2 tbs. unsalted butter
2 tbs. all purpose flour
2 cups half and half
1 cup diced cooked ham
2 tsp. lemon juice
1/4 tsp. salt
1/8 tsp. ground nutmeg
1/4 cup shredded Swiss cheese

Cut the tough woody ends off the asparagus. Trim off the outer peel. Add the asparagus to a dutch oven. Cover the asparagus with water and place over medium heat. Bring the asparagus to a boil and simmer for 10 minutes. Remove the pan from the heat and drain all the water from the asparagus.

Place the asparagus in a serving dish and keep the asparagus warm while you prepare the rest of the dish. Add the butter to the dutch oven. When the butter melts, add the all purpose flour. Stir constantly and cook for 2 minutes. Add the half and half. Stir constantly and cook until the sauce thickens and bubbles. Stir in the ham, lemon juice, salt, nutmeg and Swiss cheese. Remove the pan from the heat stir until the cheese melts. Pour the sauce over the asparagus and serve.

Asparagus in Basil Sauce

Makes 4 servings

10 oz. pkg. frozen asparagus spears
1/2 cup water
1 1/4 tsp. cornstarch
1/4 tsp. dried basil
Pinch of garlic powder
Pinch of black pepper
1/2 cup unsweetened apple juice
1 tbs. lemon juice
4 cherry tomatoes, halved

In a sauce pan over medium heat, add the asparagus and water. Place a lid on the pan and bring the asparagus to a boil. Cook for 7 minutes or until the asparagus is tender. Remove the pan from the heat and drain all the water from the pan. Place the asparagus on a serving platter and keep warm while you prepare the sauce.

Add the cornstarch, basil, garlic powder, black pepper, apple juice and lemon juice to the sauce pan. Place the pan back on the stove over medium heat. Stir constantly and cook until the sauce is thickened and smooth. Remove the pan from the heat and pour the sauce over the asparagus. Place the tomato halves over the top of the asparagus before serving.

2 SQUASH, CAULIFLOWER, TOMATOES & OTHER VEGETABLES

I love fresh squash and tomatoes. They are so easy to grow and produce in abundance in my garden. I love that most of the recipes are easy and quick to make. It is not hard to include these delicious vegetables in a fast paced life.

Spinach Stuffed Squash

Makes 6 servings

3 medium size yellow squash
3 cups water
1/4 cup unsalted butter
1 tbs. all purpose flour
1/2 cup whipping cream
1/2 tsp. salt
1/8 tsp. ground nutmeg
10 oz. pkg. frozen chopped spinach, thawed

In a large sauce pan over medium heat, add the squash and water. Bring the squash to a boil and place a lid on the pan. Cook the whole squash about 8 minutes or until the squash are tender. Remove the pan from the heat and drain all the water from the pan. Cool the squash for 10 minutes.

Cut the squash in half lengthwise. Scoop out the pulp and seeds from the center of the squash. Leave about 1/4" rim around the squash so the squash shells will stay intact. In a sauce pan over medium heat, add the butter. When the butter melts, add the all purpose flour. Stir constantly and cook for 1 minute. Add the whipping cream to the pan. Stir constantly and cook until the sauce thickens and bubbles.

Add the salt, nutmeg and spinach to the pan. Stir until well combined and cook for 3 minutes or until the spinach is hot. Remove the pan from the heat. Place the squash shells on a serving platter. Spoon the spinach filling into the squash shells and serve.

Twice Baked Squash

Makes 6 servings

3 small butternut squash, about 12 oz. each
1/3 cup sour cream
1/2 tsp. salt
1/4 tsp. ground nutmeg
6 tbs. light brown sugar

Preheat the oven to 425°. Cut the squash in half lengthwise. Scoop out the seeds and fibers. Place the squash, cut side up, in a 9 x 13 baking pan. Cover the pan with aluminum foil.

Bake for 30 minutes or until the squash is tender. Remove the squash from the oven and cool for 10 minutes. Remove the aluminum foil from the pan. Reduce the oven temperature to 375°. Scoop out the squash from the shells. Add the squash to a mixing bowl. Add the sour cream, salt, nutmeg and brown sugar to the squash. Stir until combined and spoon the filling into the squash shells. Bake for 20 minutes. Remove from the oven and serve.

Mexican Summer Vegetables

Makes 6 servings

1 tbs. olive oil
2 yellow squash, cut into 1/4" slices
1 large zucchini, cut into 1/4" slices
1 onion, peeled & thinly sliced
1 large tomato, chopped
1/2 tsp. dried oregano
1/4 tsp. salt
1/8 tsp. black pepper
1 cup taco sauce
1 cup shredded Monterey Jack cheese
1/4 cup chopped cilantro

In a large skillet over medium heat, add the olive oil. When the oil is hot, add the yellow squash and zucchini. Separate the onion into rings and add to the skillet. Saute for 5 minutes or until the squash are crisp tender.

Add the tomato and oregano to the skillet. Stir until combined and cook for 1 minute. Sprinkle the salt and black pepper over the vegetables. Add the taco sauce to the skillet. Stir until combined and cook for 3 minutes. Sprinkle the Monterey Jack cheese and cilantro over the vegetables. Remove the skillet from the heat and serve.

Curry Butternut Squash

Makes 12 servings

2 lb. butternut squash, peeled & seeded
3 tbs. melted unsalted butter
1 tsp. curry powder
1/4 tsp. salt

Cut the butternut squash into 1" cubes. Preheat the oven to 450°. Spray a 9 x 13 baking pan with non stick cooking spray. Add the squash to the baking pan. In a small bowl, add the butter, curry powder and salt. Stir until combined and drizzle over the squash. Toss until the squash is coated in the seasoned oil. Bake for 25 minutes or until the squash is tender and lightly browned. Remove from the oven and serve.

Zucchini Bake

Makes 10 servings

1/2 cup chopped onion
3 tbs. unsalted butter
6 cups chopped zucchini
1 cup cooked rice
1 cup shredded Swiss cheese
1/2 cup chopped fresh parsley
1/2 tsp. salt
1/8 tsp. black pepper
1 beaten egg
2 tbs. dry breadcrumbs
1 tbs. melted unsalted butter

Spray a 1 1/2 quart casserole dish with non stick cooking spray. Preheat the oven to 375°. In a large skillet over medium heat, add the onion and 3 tablespoons butter. Saute for 5 minutes. Add the zucchini to the skillet. Place a lid on the skillet and reduce the heat to low. Stir occasionally and simmer for 10 minutes. Remove the skillet from the heat. Cool for 10 minutes.

Add the rice, Swiss cheese, parsley, salt, black pepper and egg to the skillet. Stir until combined and spoon into the casserole dish. Sprinkle the breadcrumbs over the top. Drizzle 1 tablespoon melted butter over the breadcrumbs. Bake for 25 minutes or until hot and bubbly. Remove from the oven and serve.

Roasted Fennel And Summer Squash

Makes 4 servings

2 small fennel bulbs
3 cups chopped yellow squash
1 cup chopped onion
2 tbs. olive oil
1 tsp. black pepper
1/2 tsp. salt

Remove the stalk from the fennel bulbs. Cut the bulbs into 1/2" wedges. Chop 2 tablespoons of the fronds and set aside. In a mixing bowl, add the fennel wedges, squash, onion, olive oil, black pepper and salt. Toss until well combined and the vegetables are coated in the oil and seasonings.

Preheat the oven to 450°. Lightly spray a roasting pan with non stick cooking spray. Spoon the vegetables into the pan. Bake for 25 minutes. Stir the vegetables. Bake for 15 minutes or until the vegetables are tender and lightly browned. Remove from the oven and sprinkle the fronds over the top before serving.

Acorn Squash With Raisin Spice Sauce

Makes 4 servings

2 small acorn squash, halved lengthwise & seeded
1/4 cup orange juice
2 tbs. raisins
1/8 tsp. ground nutmeg
Salt and black pepper to taste
4 tsp. unsalted butter

Preheat the oven to 400°. Place the squash halves, cut side up, in a 9 x 13 baking pan. In a small bowl, add the orange juice, raisins, nutmeg and salt and black pepper to taste. Stir until combined and spoon over the squash.

Place 1 teaspoon butter in the center of each squash half. Fill the baking pan with water up to a 1" depth on the pan. Cover the pan with aluminum foil. Bake for 30 minutes. Remove the aluminum foil. Bake for 30 minutes or until the squash is tender. Remove from the oven and serve.

Maple Glazed Squash

Makes 6 servings

2 medium acorn squash
Salt and black pepper to taste
1 cup maple syrup
1 apple, peeled, cored and chopped
1 tsp. ground cinnamon

Cut the squash into 1" rings. Remove the seeds. Spray a 9 x 13 baking pan with non stick cooking spray. Place the squash in the baking pan. Sprinkle with salt and black pepper to taste.

In a small bowl, add the maple syrup, apple and cinnamon. Stir until combined and spoon over the squash. Preheat the oven to 350°. Bake for 50 minutes or until the squash is tender. Remove from the oven and serve.

Bacon Squash Saute

Makes 4 servings

6 bacon slices, diced
2 zucchini, cut into 1/4" slices
2 yellow squash, cut into 1/4" slices
1 onion, thinly sliced

In a large skillet over medium heat, add the bacon. Cook for 6 minutes or until the bacon is crisp. Remove the bacon from the skillet and drain on paper towels. Drain off all but 2 tablespoons bacon drippings.

Add the zucchini, yellow squash and onion to the skillet. Saute for 6 minutes or until the squash are crisp tender. Remove the skillet from the heat and sprinkle the bacon over the top.

Sauteed Squash & Tomatoes

Makes 8 servings

3 bacon slices
1 cup chopped onion
3 garlic cloves, minced
1 tbs. chopped fresh thyme
1 tsp. chopped fresh oregano
1 bay leaf
4 cups sliced zucchini
4 cups sliced yellow squash
2 cups cherry tomatoes, halved
2 tbs. unsalted butter
1 tbs. red wine vinegar
Salt and black pepper to taste

In a large skillet over medium heat, add the bacon. Cook for 6 minutes or until the bacon is crisp. Remove the bacon from the skillet and drain on paper towels. Crumble the bacon.

Add the onion, garlic, thyme, oregano and bay leaf to the skillet. Saute for 5 minutes. Add the zucchini and yellow squash to the skillet. Saute for 10 minutes. Add the cherry tomatoes to the skillet. Saute for 10 minutes. Add the butter and red wine vinegar to the skillet. Stir until combined and the butter melts. Remove the skillet from the heat and season to taste with salt and black pepper.

Zucchini Latkes

Makes 16 latkes

4 1/2 cups shredded zucchini
1 tsp. salt
2 beaten eggs
1/4 cup dry breadcrumbs
1/8 tsp. black pepper
Vegetable oil for frying

In a mixing bowl, add the zucchini and 1/2 teaspoon salt. Toss until combined. Let the zucchini sit for 10 minutes. Drain off any liquid and pat the zucchini dry with paper towels.

Add the eggs, 1/2 teaspoon salt, breadcrumbs and black pepper to the bowl. Stir until combined. In a skillet over medium heat, add vegetable oil to a 1/2" depth in the skillet. You will need to cook the latkes in batches.

When the oil is hot, drop the zucchini into the hot oil. Use about 1 tablespoon batter for each latke. Press the latkes to form into a patty with a spatula. Fry for 2 minutes on each side or until golden brown. Remove the skillet from the heat and serve.

Zucchini Parmesan Toss

Makes 4 servings

2 lbs. fresh zucchini, cut into 1/4" slices
2 tbs. olive oil
6 tbs. freshly grated Parmesan cheese
1/2 tsp. grated lemon zest
1/2 tsp. salt
1/4 tsp. black pepper

In a large skillet over medium heat, add the zucchini and olive oil. Saute for 5 minutes or until the zucchini is crisp tender. Remove the skillet from the heat. Sprinkle the Parmesan cheese, lemon zest, salt and black pepper over the zucchini. Toss until combined and serve.

Pesto Veggie Stacks

Makes 4 servings

2 cups fresh basil leaves
1/2 cup grated Parmesan cheese
1/4 cup chopped walnuts
2 tbs. grated Romano cheese
3 garlic cloves, peeled
1/2 cup plus 3 tbs. olive oil
1/4 cup all purpose flour
2 beaten eggs
1/2 cup dry breadcrumbs
8 slices eggplant, 1/2" thick
4 slices fresh tomatoes, 1/2" thick
1/4 cup crumbled feta cheese

In a blender, add the basil, Parmesan cheese, walnut, Romano cheese and garlic. Process until blended. With the blender running, slowly add 1/2 cup olive oil. Process until smooth and combined.

In a small shallow bowl, add the all purpose flour. Add the eggs to a small bowl. Add the breadcrumbs to a small bowl. Dip the eggplant slices in the all purpose flour. Dip the eggplant in the egg allowing the excess liquid to drip off back into the bowl. Dredge the eggplant in the breadcrumbs.

In a large skillet over medium heat, add 3 tablespoons olive oil. When the oil is hot, add the eggplant slices. Cook about 3 minutes on each side or until golden brown and the eggplant is tender. Remove the skillet from the heat and drain the eggplant on paper towels.

Preheat the oven to 350°. Place 4 eggplant slices on a baking sheet. Place a tomato slice over each eggplant. Sprinkle the feta cheese over the tomatoes. Spoon 2 teaspoons pesto over each tomato. You will not use all the pesto sauce. Refrigerate for another use. Place the remaining eggplant slices over the top. Bake for 8 minutes or until hot. Remove from the oven and serve.

Vegetarian Paella

Makes 6 servings

2 tsp. canola oil
1 cup chopped onion
2 garlic cloves, minced
2 1/4 cups vegetable broth
14 oz. can stewed tomatoes
1 1/4 cups zucchini, cut into 1/2" slices
1 cup dry brown rice
1 cup chopped carrots
1 cup chopped red bell pepper
1 tsp. dried Italian seasoning
1/2 tsp. ground turmeric
1/8 tsp. cayenne pepper
14 oz. can artichoke hearts, drained & quartered
1/2 cup frozen green peas
3/4 tsp. salt

In a large skillet over medium heat, add the canola oil. When the oil is hot, add the onion. Saute for 5 minutes. Add the garlic to the skillet. Saute for 2 minutes. Remove the skillet from the heat and spoon into a 5 quart slow cooker.

Add the vegetable broth, stewed tomatoes, zucchini, brown rice, carrots, red bell pepper, Italian seasoning, turmeric and cayenne pepper to the slow cooker. Stir until combined.

Set the temperature to low. Cook for 4 hours or until the rice is tender and most of the liquid absorbed. Add the artichokes, green peas and salt to the slow cooker. Stir until combined. Cook for 10 minutes or until the green peas are tender.

Grilled Vegetable Packets

Makes 4 servings

2 ears fresh corn, husked & silked
4 new potatoes, halved
2 carrots, cut into 1" chunks
1 zucchini, cut into 1" chunks
1 onion, cut into thin wedges
1/4 cup melted unsalted butter
2 tbs. Dijon mustard
1/2 tsp. dried thyme
1/4 tsp. salt
1/4 tsp. black pepper

Have your grill hot and ready. Cut each ear of corn in half. Cut four 18" x 12" pieces aluminum foil. In a mixing bowl, add the corn, new potatoes, carrots, zucchini and onion.

In a small bowl, add the butter, Dijon mustard, thyme, salt and black pepper. Stir until combined and pour over the vegetables. Toss until the vegetables are coated in the seasonings. Divide the vegetables among the four pieces aluminum foil. Place the vegetables in the center of the foil. Fold the foil to form a packet.

Place the packets on the grill. Cook for 25 minutes or until the vegetables are tender. Remove from the grill and serve. Be careful when opening the packets as hot steam will escape.

Grilled Teriyaki Vegetable Packets

Makes 4 servings

2 cups fresh baby carrots
2 cups frozen sugar snap peas
1 red bell pepper, cut into 8 wedges
1/4 cup teriyaki sauce
1/8 tsp. ground ginger
1/4 cup chopped fresh cilantro

Have your grill hot and ready. Cut four 18" x 12" pieces aluminum foil. In a mixing bowl, add the carrots, sugar snap peas and red bell pepper. Pour the teriyaki sauce over the vegetables. Sprinkle the ginger over the vegetables. Toss until the vegetables are coated in the sauce. Divide the vegetables among the four pieces aluminum foil. Place the vegetables in the center of the foil. Fold the foil to form a packet.

Place the packets on the grill. Cook for 20 minutes or until the vegetables are tender. Remove from the grill and sprinkle the cilantro over the vegetables. Be careful when opening the packets as hot steam will escape.

Braised Leeks

Makes 4 servings

6 medium leeks
2 tbs. unsalted butter
3/4 cup water
1/4 cup freshly grated Parmesan cheese
1/4 tsp. salt
1/4 tsp. black pepper

Remove the tough outer leaves, root and all but 2" of the tops from the leeks. Wash the leeks thoroughly and pat dry with paper towels. Cut into 2" pieces.

In a skillet over medium heat, add the butter. When the butter melts, add the leeks. Place a lid on the skillet and cook for 10 minutes. Stir occasionally while the leeks are cooking. Add the water to the skillet. Place the lid back on the skillet and reduce the heat to low. Stir occasionally and cook for 20 minutes or until the leeks are tender.

Remove the skillet and drain off any water. Sprinkle the Parmesan cheese, salt and black pepper over the leeks and serve.

Caramelized Onions

Makes 4 servings

2 lbs. onions, peeled
1 tbs. chopped fresh parsley
1 tbs. chopped fresh chives
1 tbs. chopped fresh thyme
1 tsp. salt
1/2 tsp. black pepper
1 tbs. unsalted butter
1 tbs. olive oil

Cut the onions into 1/4" thick slices. Separate the onions into rings. Add the onions, parsley, chives, thyme, salt and black pepper to a mixing bowl. Toss until combined.

In a large skillet over medium heat, add the butter and olive oil. When the butter melts and the oil is hot, add the onions. Saute for 25 minutes or until the onions are browned and tender. Remove from the heat and serve.

Roasted Leeks, Potatoes & Carrots

Makes 8 servings

3 medium leeks
1 lb. carrots, peeled & cut into 2" pieces
2 lbs. new potatoes, washed & quartered
1/4 cup olive oil
1 garlic clove, minced
1/2 tsp. salt
1/2 tsp. black pepper

Remove the roots and tough outer leaves from the leeks. Remove the tops except for 4". Wash the leeks thoroughly and pat dry with paper towels. Cut into 1" slices.

Spray a roasting pan with non stick cooking spray. Add the leeks, carrots and potatoes to the pan. Drizzle the olive oil over the vegetables. Sprinkle the garlic, salt and black pepper over the vegetables. Toss until the vegetables are coated in the oil and seasonings.

Preheat the oven to 450°. Bake for 45 minutes or until the vegetables are tender. Remove from the oven and serve.

Carrots & Broccoli With Orange Browned Butter

Makes 8 servings

1 lb. fresh baby carrots
1 lb. pkg. frozen broccoli florets
1/3 cup unsalted butter
1 tsp. grated orange zest
1/2 tsp. grated fresh ginger
2 tbs. orange juice

Add the carrots to a sauce pan over medium heat. Cover the carrots with water and bring to a boil. Reduce the heat to low and place a lid on the pan. Cook for 3 minutes.

Add the broccoli to the pan. Cook for 5 minutes or until the carrots and broccoli are crisp tender. Remove the pan from the heat and drain all the water from the vegetables.

In a small sauce pan over medium heat, add the butter. Cook until the butter turns golden brown. Remove the pan from the heat and add the orange zest, ginger and orange juice. Stir until combined and pour over the broccoli and carrots. Toss until combined and serve.

Ginger Lime Carrots

Makes 4 servings

1 lb. carrots, cut into 1/2" slices
1 tbs. lime juice
1 tbs. unsalted butter
1 tbs. honey
1 tsp. grated lime zest
1/4 tsp. ground ginger

In a sauce pan over medium heat, add the carrots. Cover the carrots with water and bring to a boil. Reduce the heat to low and place a lid on the pan. Simmer for 10 minutes or until the carrots are crisp tender. Remove the pan from the heat and drain all the water from the carrots.

Place the pan back on the stove. Add the lime juice, butter, honey, lime zest and ginger to the carrots. Stir until combined. Cook for 2 minutes or until combined and the glaze hot. Remove from the heat and serve.

Roasted Italian Vegetables

Makes 4 servings

1 zucchini, cut into 1/4" slices
1 1/2 cups sliced baby portobello mushrooms
1 orange bell pepper, julienned
1 tbs. olive oil
1 tbs. melted unsalted butter
1 tsp. dried Italian seasoning
1/2 tsp. salt
1/8 tsp. black pepper

Add all the ingredients to a mixing bowl. Toss until the vegetables are coated in the oil and seasonings. Preheat the oven to 450°. Spray a large baking sheet with non stick cooking spray.

Place the vegetables on the baking sheet. Bake for 15 minutes or until the vegetables are tender. Stir every 5 minutes to ensure even roasting. Remove the vegetables from the oven and serve.

Roasted Root Vegetables

Makes 12 servings

2 lbs. carrots, peeled and cut into 1" pieces
2 lbs. parsnips, peeled and cut into 1" pieces
2 large red onions, peeled and cut into 1" wedges
1/2 cup olive oil
1 tbs. salt
1/2 tsp. black pepper

Line two large baking sheets with aluminum foil. Preheat the oven to 425°. Add all the ingredients to a large bowl. Toss until the vegetables are coated in the oil and seasonings. Spread the vegetables on the baking pans.

Bake for 30 minutes. Stir the vegetables and bake for 10 minutes or until the vegetables are tender and browned. Remove from the oven and serve.

Pepper Parsnip Fries

Makes 8 servings

8 medium parsnips, peeled
1 tbs. olive oil
1/4 cup grated Parmesan cheese
12 tsp. salt
1/4 tsp. black pepper
1/8 tsp. ground nutmeg

Preheat the oven to 425°. Line two 15 x 10 x 1 baking pans with aluminum foil. Spray the aluminum foil with non stick cooking spray. Cut the parsnips into french fry size pieces. Add the olive oil, Parmesan cheese, salt, black pepper and nutmeg to a large Ziploc bag. Close the bag and shake until combined.

Add the parsnip fries, a few at a time, to the bag. Shake until the fries are coated in the seasonings. Place the fries on the baking sheets in a single layer. Stir occasionally and bake for 25 minutes or until the fries are tender and golden brown. Remove from the oven and serve.

Roasted Parsnips & Apples

Makes 8 servings

2 lbs. parsnips, peeled and cut lengthwise into quarters
2 lbs. Fuji apples, peeled, cored and quartered
2 tbs. chopped fresh sage
3 tbs. olive oil
1 tsp. salt
1/2 tsp. black pepper
1/8 tsp. ground nutmeg
1/8 tsp. ground allspice

Preheat the oven to 475°. Spray a large baking pan with non stick cooking spray. Add all the ingredients to a mixing bowl. Toss until apples and parsnips are coated in the oil and seasonings. Spread on the baking pan.

Bake for 30 minutes or until the apples and parsnips are tender. Stir occasionally while baking. Remove from the oven and serve.

Parsnip Sweet Potato Patties

Makes 2 dozen

1 cup all purpose flour
3 tbs. minced fresh thyme
2 tsp. salt
1/4 tsp. black pepper
4 beaten eggs
2 lbs. sweet potatoes, peeled & grated
1 lb. parsnips, peeled & grated
12 green onions, sliced
1/2 cup vegetable oil

In a large bowl, add the all purpose flour, thyme, salt and black pepper. Stir until combined. Add the eggs to the bowl. Stir until combined. Add the sweet potatoes, parsnips and green onions to the bowl. Stir until combined.

You will need to cook the patties in batches. In a large skillet over medium heat, add the vegetable oil. When the oil is hot, add the patties. Use about 1/4 cup batter for each patty. Fry for 3 minutes on each side or until tender and golden brown. Remove the patties from the skillet and drain on paper towels.

Roasted Beets

Makes 4 servings

2 lbs. baby beets, trimmed and washed
4 tbs. unsalted butter, cut into small pieces
1 cup vegetable broth
1/4 cup honey
2 tbs. cider vinegar
3 fresh thyme sprigs
3 fresh parsley sprigs
1/8 tsp. salt
1/8 tsp. black pepper
1 tbs. olive oil

Preheat the oven to 350°. Place the beets in a 11 x 7 baking pan. Place the butter over the beets. In a small bowl, add the vegetable broth, honey, cider vinegar, thyme sprigs, parsley sprigs, salt and black pepper. Whisk until combined and pour over the beets.

Cover the pan with aluminum foil. Bake for 1 hour or until the beets are tender. Remove the pan from the oven. Cool the beets for 15 minutes. Peel the beets and cut into quarters. In a large skillet over medium heat, add the olive oil. When the oil is hot, add the beets. Saute for 4 minutes or until the beets are lightly browned. Remove the skillet from the heat and serve.

Ginger Orange Beets

Makes 4 servings

4 medium beets, trimmed & cleaned
6 tbs. olive oil
1/4 tsp. salt
1/4 tsp. white pepper
1 tbs. rice wine vinegar
1 tbs. frozen orange juice concentrate
1 1/2 tsp. grated orange zest
1/2 tsp. minced fresh ginger
1 orange, peeled & chopped
1/3 cup toasted pecan halves

Brush the beets with 4 tablespoons olive oil. Sprinkle the salt and white pepper over the beets. Wrap the beets loosely in aluminum foil. Preheat the oven to 425°. Place the beets on a baking pan. Bake for 1 to 1 1/4 hours or until the beets are tender. Remove from the oven and cool for 10 minutes.

In a small bowl, add the rice wine vinegar, orange juice concentrate, orange zest and ginger. Whisk until combined. Peel the beets and cut into wedges. Add the beets and orange to a serving bowl. Pour the dressing over the top. Gently toss until combined. Sprinkle the pecans over the top and serve.

Roasted Turnips With Honey Butter

Makes 4 servings

3 tbs. unsalted butter
3 tbs. honey
2 lbs. fresh turnips, washed, peeled & cubed
1 tsp. salt
1/2 tsp. black pepper
1/4 cup chopped fresh parsley

Preheat the oven to 400°. Line a large baking sheet with aluminum foil. In a microwavable bowl, add the butter and honey. Microwave for 30 seconds or until the butter melts. Remove the bowl from the microwave and stir until combined.

Place the turnips on the baking sheet. Sprinkle the salt and black pepper over the turnips. Drizzle the honey butter over the turnips. Toss until the turnips are coated in the honey butter.

Bake for 35 minutes or until golden brown. Stir occasionally while baking for even cooking. Remove from the oven and spoon the turnips into a serving bowl. Sprinkle the parsley over the top and serve.

Sorghum Glazed Turnips

Makes 4 servings

2 small turnips, peeled and halved
1 1/2 cups plus 3 tbs. water
2 tbs. unsalted butter
1 tbs. lemon juice
1 1/2 tsp. granulated sugar
1/2 tsp. salt
2 tsp. sorghum molasses

In a cast iron skillet over medium heat, add the turnips, 1 1/2 cups water, butter, lemon juice, granulated sugar and salt. Stir until combined and bring to a boil. Place a lid on the skillet. Stir occasionally and simmer for 10 minutes.

Remove the lid from the skillet. Stir occasionally and cook for 5 minutes or until the turnips are tender and the water has evaporated. Stir constantly and cook for 5 minutes or until the turnips are golden brown. Add the sorghum molasses and 3 tablespoons water to the skillet. Stir until well combined and the turnips are coated in the glaze. Remove the skillet from the heat and serve.

Tomato Corn Risotto

Makes 5 servings

2 1/2 cups water
2 cups whole milk
3 tbs. chicken broth
1 1/4 cups finely chopped onion
2 garlic cloves, minced
2 tbs. unsalted butter
3/4 cup dry arborio rice
1 1/3 cups fresh corn kernels
1 cup diced tomato
1/2 cup grated Parmesan cheese
1/2 cup fresh basil leaves, thinly sliced
1/2 tsp. salt
Black pepper to taste

In a large sauce pan over medium heat, add the water, milk and chicken broth. Cook only until the broth is warm. Do not let the liquids boil. Keep the liquids warm while you cook the recipe.

In a large skillet over medium heat, add the onion, garlic and butter. Saute for 5 minutes. Add the rice to the skillet. Saute for 3 minutes. Add 1 cup hot broth to the skillet. Stir until the liquid is absorbed.

Add the remaining broth, 1/2 cup at a time, to the skillet. Do not add additional broth until each 1/2 cup has been absorbed. Stir constantly while cooking the risotto. This takes about 20 minutes on my stove. The liquid should be absorbed and the rice tender when ready.

Add the corn, tomato, Parmesan cheese, basil and salt to the skillet. Stir until combined and cook only until thoroughly heated. Remove the skillet from the heat and season to taste with black pepper.

Smoky Grilled Corn

Makes 6 servings

2 tbs. plus 1 1/2 tsp. unsalted butter
1/2 cup honey
2 garlic cloves, minced
2 tbs. Tabasco sauce
1/2 tsp. salt
1/4 tsp. black pepper
1/4 tsp. paprika
6 ears fresh corn, husk and silk removed

In a small sauce pan over medium heat, add the butter. When the butter melts, add the honey, garlic, Tabasco sauce, salt, black pepper and paprika. Stir until combined and the sauce is hot. Remove the pan from the heat.

Have your grill hot and ready. Brush the butter sauce over the corn. Place the corn on the grill over medium coals. Close the grill lid. Turn occasionally and cook about 12 minutes or until the corn is tender. Baste the corn with the remaining butter while cooking. Remove the corn from the grill and serve.

Corn Stuffed Peppers

Makes 6 servings

1 1/2 cups canned whole kernel corn, drained
1 cup shredded cheddar cheese
1/2 cup sliced black olives
2 tbs. chopped green chiles
2 tbs. chopped green onion
Salt and black pepper to taste
3 large green bell peppers

Preheat the oven to 350°. In a mixing bowl, add the corn, cheddar cheese, black olives, green chiles and green onion. Stir until combined and season to taste with salt and black pepper.

Cut the green bell peppers in half. Remove the stem, seeds and membrane. Place the peppers in a 9 x 13 baking pan. Spoon the corn filling into the peppers. Cover the pan with aluminum foil.

Bake for 30 minutes or until the peppers are tender and the filling hot. Remove from the oven and serve.

Cheese Stuffed Peppers

Makes 8 servings

2 red bell peppers
2 yellow bell peppers
4 oz. crumbled goat cheese
1 tbs. chopped fresh chives
1 tbs. chopped fresh basil
1 garlic clove, minced

Cut the peppers in half lengthwise. Remove the seeds and membrane. Place the peppers, cut side down, on a baking sheet. Turn the oven to the broiler position. Broil for 5-8 minutes or until the skins blister and are blackened. Remove from the oven.

Dampen several paper towels and wrap the peppers in the paper towels. Place in a Ziploc bag and let rest for 10 minutes. Remove the skins from the peppers and discard.

In a small bowl, add the goat cheese, chives, basil and garlic. Stir until combined. Place the peppers back on the baking sheet. Turn the oven to the broiler position. Spoon the cheese filling into the peppers.

Broil for 2-3 minutes or until the cheese melts and is bubbly. Remove from the oven and serve.

Southwest Sweet Corn And Zucchini

Makes 4 servings

2 cups chopped zucchini
1/2 cup chopped onion
3 tbs. unsalted butter
2 cups fresh corn kernels
1/4 cup chopped fresh chives
2 tsp. taco seasoning mix

In a large skillet over medium heat, add the zucchini, onion and butter. Saute for 5 minutes. Add the corn, chives and taco seasoning to the skillet. Stir constantly and cook for 5 minutes or until the corn is tender. Remove the skillet from the heat and serve.

Poached Corn

Makes 6 servings

5 cups frozen whole kernel corn
2 cups whole milk
4 tsp. granulated sugar
1 tbs. unsalted butter
3/4 tsp. salt
1/2 tsp. black pepper

Add all the ingredients to a sauce pan over medium low heat. Stir until combined. Stir frequently and cook about 10 minutes or until the corn is tender. Remove the pan from the heat and drain off the liquid. Serve hot.

Fresh Corn Medley

Makes 5 servings

1 green bell pepper, chopped
1/2 cup chopped onion
3 tbs. unsalted butter
4 cups fresh corn kernels
1/4 cup hot water
2 oz. jar diced red pimentos, drained
1 tbs. honey
1 tsp. salt
1/8 tsp. black pepper
1/2 cup shredded cheddar cheese
4 bacon slices, cooked and crumbled

In a large skillet over medium heat, add the green bell pepper, onion and butter. Saute for 5 minutes or until the vegetables are tender. Add the corn, water, red pimentos, honey, salt and black pepper to the skillet. Stir until combined.

Bring the corn to a boil and reduce the heat to low. Stir occasionally and simmer for 10 minutes or until the corn is tender. Remove the skillet from the heat and sprinkle the cheddar cheese and bacon over the top before serving.

Garden Stir Fry

Makes 6 servings

2 tbs. olive oil
1 1/2 cups carrots, cut into 1/4" slices
1 cup broccoli florets, cut into 1" pieces
1 cup cauliflower florets, cut into 1" pieces
1 garlic clove, minced
3 tbs. water
1 1/2 cups fresh snow pea pods, trimmed
1 red bell pepper, cut into 1/4" strips
1/4 cup chopped onion
1/2 tsp. salt
1/4 tsp. dried basil
1/8 tsp. black pepper

In a large skillet over medium high heat, add the olive oil. When the oil is hot, add the carrots, broccoli, cauliflower and garlic. Stir constantly and cook for 2 minutes.

Add the water to the skillet. Place a lid on the skillet and cook for 4 minutes. Add the pea pods, red bell pepper, onion, salt, basil and black pepper to the skillet. Stir constantly and cook for 2 minutes or until all the liquid evaporates and the vegetables are tender. Remove the skillet from the heat and serve.

Fresh Tomatoes With Parsley Pesto

Makes 6 servings

1 cup packed fresh parsley
1/4 cup chopped fresh chives
1 garlic clove, peeled
1/8 tsp. black pepper
3 tbs. olive oil
2 tbs. red wine vinegar
4 large tomatoes, cut into wedges

In a food processor, add the parsley, chives, garlic and black pepper. Pulse until finely chopped. With the food processor running, slowly add the olive oil and red wine vinegar. Process until well combined. Spoon the pesto into a bowl. Cover the bowl and refrigerate for 24 hours before serving.

When ready to serve, place the tomatoes on a serving platter. Spoon the pesto over the tomatoes and serve. The pesto will keep covered in the refrigerator about 1 week.

Bean Stuffed Tomatoes

Makes 6 servings

12 oz. fresh green beans, trimmed & cut into 2" pieces
8 oz. fresh wax beans, trimmed & cut into 2" pieces
15 oz. can black beans, rinsed & drained
1 red bell pepper, cut into 1" strips
3 green onions, sliced
1/4 cup minced fresh cilantro
1/4 cup olive oil
3 tbs. red wine vinegar
1 tsp. ground cumin
1 garlic clove, minced
1/2 tsp. salt
1/4 tsp. black pepper
6 large firm ripe tomatoes

In a sauce pan over medium heat, add the green and wax beans. Cover the beans with water and bring to a boil. Cook for 8 minutes or until the beans are crisp tender. Remove the pan from the heat and drain all the water from the pan.

Add the black beans, red bell pepper, green onions and cilantro to the green beans. Stir until combined. In a small bowl, add the olive oil, red wine vinegar, cumin, garlic, salt and black pepper. Whisk until combined and pour over the beans.

Toss until combined. Cover the pan and refrigerate for 30 minutes. Cut a 1/4" slice off the top of each tomato. Scoop out the pulp from the tomatoes. Spoon the beans into the tomatoes and serve.

Onion Topped Tomatoes

Makes 12 servings

6 large fresh tomatoes
3/4 tsp. dried basil
1/8 tsp. salt
1/4 tsp. garlic powder
1/8 tsp. black pepper
12 thin onion slices
1/4 cup grated Parmesan cheese

Preheat the oven to 350°. Cut the tomatoes in half crosswise. Place the tomatoes in a 9 x 13 baking pan. Sprinkle the basil, salt, garlic powder and black pepper over the tomatoes. Place an onion slice over each tomato. Sprinkle the Parmesan cheese over the onion. Cover the pan with aluminum foil. Bake for 20 minutes. Remove the pan from the oven and serve.

Orange Marjoram Carrots

Makes 4 servings

3 cups sliced carrots
1/2 cup water
2 tbs. unsalted butter
1 tbs. orange juice
1 tbs. honey
1/8 tsp. dried marjoram

In a sauce pan over medium heat, add the carrots and water. Bring to a boil and place a lid on the pan. Simmer for 8 minutes or until the carrots are tender. Remove the pan from the heat and drain any water from the carrots.

Add the butter, orange juice, honey and marjoram to the pan. Reduce the heat to low and place the pan back on the stove. Stir constantly and cook for 3 minutes. Remove from the heat and serve.

Glazed Julienned Carrots

Makes 8 servings

2 lbs. carrots, peeled and julienned
1/3 cup unsalted butter, cubed
1/4 cup granulated sugar
1/4 cup water
1/2 tsp. salt

In a large skillet over medium heat, add all the ingredients. Stir occasionally and place a lid on the skillet. Cook about 10 minutes or until the carrots are crisp tender. Remove the skillet from the heat. Drain off the excess liquid and serve.

Carrots & Pearl Onions

Makes 4 servings

3 cups water
8 oz. fresh pearl onions, peeled
1 tbs. unsalted butter
1 1/2 tsp. granulated sugar
1 lb. carrots, peeled and cut into 1/4" slices
6 bacon slices, cooked and crumbled
1/2 cup chicken broth
1 bay leaf
1 tsp. dried thyme
1/4 tsp. salt
1/8 tsp. black pepper

Add the water to a large sauce pan over medium heat. Bring the water to a boil and add the onions. Boil for 3 minutes. Remove the pan from the heat and drain all the water from the pan. Rinse the onions with cold water and drain all the water again.

Add the butter to the pan. Place the pan back on the stove over medium heat. Sprinkle 3/4 teaspoon granulated sugar over the onions. Saute for 6 minutes or until the onions are golden brown. Add the carrots, bacon, chicken broth, bay leaf, thyme, salt, black pepper and 3/4 teaspoon granulated sugar to the sauce pan. Stir until combined.

Bring the carrots to a boil and reduce the heat to medium low. Place a lid on the pan and simmer for 10 minutes or until the carrots are tender. Remove the lid from the pan. Simmer for for 5 minutes or until the liquid reduces by half. Remove the pan from the heat and drain off the remaining liquid. Remove the bay leaf and discard. Serve hot.

Creamed Mushrooms

Makes 8 servings

3 lbs. sliced fresh mushrooms
1/2 cup unsalted butter, cubed
1/2 cup all purpose flour
2 1/2 cups whole milk
1 cup evaporated milk
2 tsp. salt

In a large sauce pan over medium heat, add the mushrooms. Cover the mushrooms with water. Bring to a boil and cook for 3 minutes or until the mushrooms are tender. Remove the pan from the heat and drain all the water from the mushrooms.

In a dutch oven over medium heat, add the butter. When the butter melts, add the all purpose flour. Stir constantly and cook for 2 minutes. Add the whole milk and evaporated milk to the pan. Stir constantly and cook about 2 minutes or until the sauce thickens. Add the mushrooms and salt to the pan. Stir until well combined and thoroughly heated. Remove the pan from the heat and serve.

Garlic Goat Cheese Stuffed Mushrooms

Makes 4 servings

12 large fresh button mushrooms
2 tbs. melted unsalted butter
4 oz. pkg. goat cheese, crumbled
2 garlic cloves, minced
2 tbs. chopped fresh parsley
1/2 tsp. dried rosemary
1/4 tsp. salt
1/4 tsp. dried basil
1/8 tsp. black pepper
2 tbs. dry white wine

Remove the stems from the mushrooms. Chop the stems and add to a skillet over medium heat. Add 1 tablespoon melted butter to the skillet. Saute for 5 minutes. Add the mushroom caps to the skillet. Saute for 2 minutes on each side. Remove the skillet from the heat. Remove the mushroom caps from the skillet and drain on paper towels.

Add the goat cheese, garlic, parsley, rosemary, salt, basil, black pepper and white wine to the skillet. Stir until combined. Preheat the oven to the broiler position. Place the mushroom caps on a baking pan. Spoon the goat cheese filling into the mushroom caps. Broil for 5 minutes or until the filling is lightly browned. Remove from the oven and serve.

Bacon & Cheese Stuffed Mushrooms

Makes 20 mushrooms

20 button mushrooms
1/2 cup shredded Swiss cheese
2 slices bacon, cooked and crumbled
1 tbs. dry breadcrumbs
1 tbs. chopped fresh parsley
1 tbs. capers, drained
Salt and black pepper to taste

Preheat the oven to 350°. Wipe the mushrooms with a damp paper towel to clean if needed. Remove the stems from the mushrooms and add to a food processor.

Add the Swiss cheese, bacon, breadcrumbs, parsley and capers to the food processor. Process until finely chopped. Season to taste with salt and black pepper. Spoon the filling into the mushroom caps. Place the mushrooms on a large baking pan. Bake for 10 minutes or until the mushrooms are tender. Remove from the oven and serve.

Sauteed Portobello Mushrooms

Makes 3 servings

3 fresh portobello mushrooms
4 garlic cloves, minced
1/4 cup olive oil
3 tbs. chopped fresh parsley
1/4 tsp. salt
1/4 tsp. black pepper

Remove the stem and gills from the mushrooms. Cut the mushrooms into 1/4" slices. Chop the stems if desired. In a large skillet over medium heat, add the garlic and olive oil. Saute for 1 minute.

Add the mushrooms to the skillet. Saute for 3 minutes or until the mushrooms are tender. Remove the skillet from the heat and sprinkle the parsley, salt and black pepper over the mushrooms. Serve hot.

Burgundy Mushrooms

Makes 4 servings

1 lb. fresh mushrooms, cleaned & halved
1/2 cup chopped onion
2 tbs. melted unsalted butter
1/2 cup dry red wine
1 tbs. Worcestershire sauce
1/4 tsp. salt
1/8 tsp. black pepper

In a skillet over medium heat, add the mushrooms, onion and butter. Saute for 4 minutes. Add the red wine, Worcestershire sauce, salt and black pepper to the skillet. Saute for 5 minutes or until most of the liquid evaporates. Remove from the heat and serve.

Goat Cheese Basil Grilled Bell Peppers

Makes 6 servings

3 large bell peppers (red, yellow or green)
3 tbs. olive oil
2 tbs. balsamic vinegar
1 tbs. light brown sugar
1/2 cup crumbled goat cheese
1/2 cup torn fresh basil leaves
Salt and black pepper to taste

Have your grill hot and ready. Cut the peppers into quarters and remove the seeds and membrane. Spray the peppers with non stick cooking spray. Place the peppers on the grill. Turn frequently and cook about 5 minutes or until the peppers are tender. Remove the peppers from the grill and place on a serving plate.

In a small bowl, add the olive oil, balsamic vinegar and brown sugar. Whisk until combined and drizzle over the peppers. Sprinkle the goat cheese and basil over the peppers. Season to taste with salt and black pepper.

Bacon Fried Okra

Makes 4 servings

8 oz. fresh okra, trimmed
2 tbs. hot bacon drippings
Salt to taste

In a skillet over medium heat, add the okra and hot bacon drippings. Stir frequently and cook for 10 minutes or until the okra is tender. Remove the skillet from the heat and sprinkle salt to taste over the okra.

Okra Skillet

Makes 8 servings

6 slices bacon
1/2 cup chopped onion
1/2 cup chopped green bell pepper
1/2 cup chopped celery
8 oz. okra, trimmed & cut into 1/2" slices
1 1/2 cups cooked whole kernel corn
1 cup chopped tomato
1 tsp. salt
1/2 tsp. dried oregano
1/4 tsp. black pepper
1/4 tsp. Tabasco sauce

In a skillet over medium heat, add the bacon. Cook for 7 minutes or until the bacon is crispy. Remove the bacon from the skillet and drain on paper towels.

Add the onion, green bell pepper, celery and okra to the skillet. Saute for 7 minutes. Add the corn, tomato, salt, oregano, black pepper and Tabasco sauce to the skillet. Stir until combined and cook for 5 minutes. Remove the skillet from the heat. Crumble the bacon and sprinkle over the top. Serve hot.

Cauliflower With Red Pepper Sauce

Makes 6 servings

1 head cauliflower, leaves removed
2 large red bell peppers
1 tsp. chopped fresh tarragon
1 tsp. salt
1/2 cup warm half and half
1/4 cup chopped fresh parsley

Remove part of the stem from the head of cauliflower. Add 1" water to a large sauce pan over medium heat. When the water is boiling, add the cauliflower. Place a lid on the pan. Cook for 15 minutes or until the cauliflower is crisp tender. Remove the pan from the heat.

While the cauliflower is cooking, make the sauce. In a large sauce pan over medium heat, add the whole red bell peppers. Cover the peppers with water and bring to a boil. Boil for 10 minutes or until the skins loosens on the peppers. Remove the pan from the heat and drain all the water from the peppers. Rinse the peppers in cold water. Remove the skins, stem, seeds and membranes from the peppers.

Chop the peppers and add to a food processor. Add the tarragon and salt to the food processor. Process until smooth. With the food processor running, slowly add the half and half. Process until combined.

Place the cauliflower on a serving platter. Spoon the sauce over the cauliflower. Sprinkle the parsley over the top and serve.

Cauliflower With Raspberry Vinaigrette

Makes 6 servings

3 cups cauliflower florets
1/4 cup olive oil
2 tbs. chopped fresh parsley
1 tbs. raspberry vinegar
2 tsp. raspberry jelly
1/4 tsp. salt
1/4 tsp. black pepper

In a sauce pan over medium heat, add the cauliflower. Cover the cauliflower with water and bring to a boil. Cook about 6 minutes or until the cauliflower is crisp tender. Remove the pan from the heat and spoon the cauliflower into a serving bowl.

While the cauliflower is cooking, make the vinaigrette. In a jar with a lid, add the olive oil, parsley, raspberry vinegar, raspberry jelly, salt and black pepper. Place the lid on the jar and shake until combined. Pour over the cauliflower. Toss until the cauliflower is coated in the vinaigrette. Serve hot.

Curry Potatoes, Cauliflower & Green Peas

Makes 6 servings

1 tbs. vegetable oil
1 cup chopped onion
2 tbs. minced fresh ginger
2 garlic cloves, chopped
2 lbs. unpeeled red potatoes, cut into 1/2" slices
1 tsp. garam marsala
1 tsp. salt
1 1/4 lb. head cauliflower, cut into florets
1 cup vegetable broth
2 plum tomatoes, seeded & chopped
1 cup chopped green peas

If you do not have garam marsala spice, substitute 1/2 teaspoon ground cumin and 1/2 teaspoon ground coriander for the spice. In a large skillet over medium heat, add the vegetable oil, onion, ginger and garlic. Saute for 5 minutes. Remove the skillet from the heat.

Add the potatoes to a 4 quart slow cooker. Sprinkle 1/2 the garam marsala and 1/2 the salt over the potatoes. Spoon the onions over the potatoes. Spoon the cauliflower over the onions and potatoes. Sprinkle the remaining garam marsala and salt over the top. Pour the vegetable broth over the vegetables. Do not stir.

Set the temperature to high. Cook for 3 1/2 hours. Add the plum tomatoes and green peas to the slow cooker. Gently stir until combined.

Cheesy Slow Cooker Cauliflower

Makes 8 servings

3 lbs. cauliflower florets
1/4 cup water
5 tbs. unsalted butter
1 cup finely chopped onion
6 tbs. all purpose flour
1/4 tsp. dry mustard
2 cups whole milk
2 cups shredded sharp cheddar cheese
1/2 tsp. salt
1/4 tsp. black pepper

Spray a 5 quart slow cooker with non stick cooking spray. Add the cauliflower and water to the slow cooker. In a skillet over medium heat, add the butter and onion. Saute for 5 minutes. Add the all purpose flour to the skillet. Stir constantly and cook for 2 minutes. Add the dry mustard and milk to the skillet. Stir constantly and cook about 5 minutes or until the sauce thickens and bubbles.

Remove the skillet from the heat. Add the cheddar cheese, salt and black pepper to the sauce. Stir until combined and pour over the cauliflower. Stir until combined. Set the temperature to low. Cook for 4 hours or until the cauliflower is tender.

Maple Vegetable Medley

Makes 8 servings

1/3 cup balsamic vinegar
1/3 cup maple syrup
1 large red onion, peeled
1 lb. fresh asparagus, trimmed
1 lb. baby carrots
2 zucchini, cut lengthwise into thirds
1 red bell pepper, seeded & cut into 8 wedges
1 yellow bell pepper, seeded & cut into 8 wedges
2 tbs. olive oil
1 tsp. dried thyme
1/2 tsp. salt
1/2 tsp. black pepper

In a small sauce pan over medium heat, add the balsamic vinegar and maple syrup. Stir until combined and bring to a boil. Cook for 5 minutes or until the glaze thickens. Remove the pan from the heat and set aside for the moment.

The onion needs to remain intact. Cut the onion into 8 wedges but do not cut all the way through. Add the onion, asparagus, carrots, zucchini, red bell pepper and yellow bell pepper to a large bowl. Drizzle the olive oil over the vegetables. Sprinkle the thyme, salt and black pepper over the vegetables. Toss until combined.

You can grill or roast the veggies. To grill the veggies, have your grill hot and ready. Spray your grill rack with non stick cooking spray. Place the veggies on the rack. Cook for 10 minutes on each side. Brush the glaze over the veggies. Cook for 5 minutes or until the veggies are tender. Remove from the grill and serve.

To roast the veggies, preheat the oven to 400°. Spread the veggies on a large baking sheet. Bake for 30 minutes or until the veggies are almost tender. Brush the glaze over the veggies. Bake for 10 minutes or until the veggies are lightly browned and tender. Remove from the oven and serve.

3 CASSEROLES

Vegetables are a mainstay in casseroles. They not only add great flavor to a casserole but they allow you to sneak in additional vegetables to your menu.

Cauliflower Gratin

Makes 6 servings

1/4 cup unsalted butter
2 1/2 lb. head cauliflower, separated into florets
1 cup chopped onion
2 garlic cloves, minced
2 tbs. all purpose flour
2 tsp. chopped fresh thyme
1/2 tsp. salt
1/2 cup whipping cream
1 cup shredded Gruyere cheese
2/3 cup panko breadcrumbs
1/4 cup sliced almonds
1/4 cup grated Parmesan cheese

Preheat the oven to 400°. In a large skillet over medium heat, add the butter, cauliflower, onion and garlic. Saute for 10 minutes or until the cauliflower browns and is crisp tender. Sprinkle the all purpose flour, thyme and salt over the cauliflower. Stir until well combined. Remove the skillet from the heat.

Spoon the cauliflower into a 11 x 7 casserole dish. Drizzle the whipping cream over the top of the cauliflower. Sprinkle the Gruyere cheese, breadcrumbs, almonds and Parmesan cheese over the top. Bake for 15-20 minutes or until the cauliflower is tender and the top golden brown. Remove the dish from the oven and serve.

Sun Dried Tomato Cauliflower Casserole

Makes 4 servings

3 tbs. olive oil
8 sun dried tomatoes, cut into thin strips
2 garlic cloves, minced
4 oz. can diced green chiles, drained
2 pkgs. thawed frozen cauliflower in cheese sauce, 10 oz. size
1/4 cup plain breadcrumbs
1/4 cup grated Parmesan cheese

In a skillet over medium heat, add the olive oil. When the oil is hot, add the tomatoes, garlic and green chiles. Stir constantly and cook for 2 minutes. Remove the skillet from the heat and spoon into a 9" deep dish pie pan.

Spoon the cauliflower and cheese sauce over the tomatoes in the pie pan. Sprinkle the breadcrumbs and Parmesan cheese over the top. Preheat the oven to 400°. Bake for 20 minutes or until bubbly and the cauliflower tender. Remove from the oven and serve.

Green Bean Tomato Bake

Makes 12 servings

3 lbs. fresh green beans, trimmed & cut into 2" pieces
5 cups diced fresh tomatoes
3 cups sliced fresh mushrooms
1 cup chopped onion
10 tbs. unsalted butter
1 1/2 tsp. minced garlic
1 1/2 tsp. dried basil
1 1/2 tsp. dried oregano
1 1/2 cups soft breadcrumbs
1/3 cup grated Parmesan cheese

In a sauce pan over medium heat, add the green beans. Cover the beans with water and bring to a boil. Cook for 8 minutes or until the green beans are crisp tender. Remove the pan from the heat and drain all the water from the green beans. Add the tomatoes to the pan and stir until combined.

In a skillet over medium heat, add the mushrooms, onion and 4 tablespoons butter. Saute for 5 minutes. Add 1 teaspoon garlic, 1 teaspoon basil and 1 teaspoon oregano to the skillet. Saute for 2 minutes. Add the green beans and tomatoes to the skillet. Stir until combined and remove the skillet from the heat.

Preheat the oven to 400°. Spray a 9 x 13 baking dish with non stick cooking spray. Spoon the casserole into the dish. In a skillet over medium heat, add 6 tablespoons butter. When the butter melts, add the breadcrumbs, Parmesan cheese, 1/2 teaspoon garlic, 1/2 teaspoon basil and 1/2 teaspoon oregano. Toss until combined and the breadcrumbs are coated in the butter and seasonings. Remove the skillet from the heat and sprinkle the breadcrumbs over the casserole.

Cover the dish with aluminum foil. Bake for 20 minutes. Remove the aluminum foil from the dish. Bake for 15 minutes or until bubbly and golden brown. Remove from the oven and serve.

Buttery Vegetable Gratin

Makes 12 servings

3 leeks, halved lengthwise & cut into 1" pieces
1 red bell pepper, cut into 1/2" pieces
5 tbs. unsalted butter
1/4 cup grated Parmesan cheese
1 tsp. chopped fresh thyme
3/4 tsp. salt
1/4 tsp. black pepper
2 large zucchini, cut into 3/4" slices
2 large yellow squash, cut into 3/4" slices
1 1/2 cups fresh breadcrumbs

Spray a 5 quart slow cooker with non stick cooking spray. Add the leek and red bell pepper to the slow cooker. Cut 1 tablespoon butter into small pieces and place over the vegetables. Sprinkle 1 tablespoon Parmesan cheese, 1/2 teaspoon thyme, 1/4 teaspoon salt and 1/8 teaspoon black pepper over the vegetables.

Place the zucchini over the top. Cut 1 tablespoon butter into small pieces and place over the vegetables. Sprinkle 1 tablespoon Parmesan cheese, 1/2 teaspoon thyme, 1/4 teaspoon salt and 1/8 teaspoon black pepper over the vegetables.

Place the yellow squash over the top. Cut 1 tablespoon butter into small pieces and place over the vegetables. Sprinkle 2 tablespoons Parmesan cheese and 1/4 teaspoon salt over the squash. Set the temperature to low and cook for 4-5 hours or until the vegetables are tender.

In a skillet over medium heat, add 2 tablespoons butter. When the butter melts, add the breadcrumbs. Saute for 5 minutes or until the breadcrumbs are toasted. Sprinkle over the vegetables and serve.

Old Fashioned Squash Casserole

Makes 6 servings

2 lbs. yellow squash, sliced
1 cup finely chopped onion
2 tbs. unsalted butter, melted
1 1/2 cups Ritz cracker crumbs
1 1/2 cups shredded sharp cheddar cheese
2 beaten eggs
4 bacon slices, cooked and crumbled
2 oz. jar diced red pimento, drained
1/4 tsp. salt
1/4 tsp. black pepper

Add the squash to a sauce pan over medium heat. Cover the squash with water and bring to a boil. Place a lid on the pan and reduce the heat to low. Simmer for 8 minutes or until the squash is tender. Remove the pan from the heat and drain all the liquid from the pan. Mash the squash with a fork or potato masher.

In a skillet over medium heat, add the onion and butter. Saute for 4 minutes. Remove the skillet from the heat. Add the squash, 3/4 cup cracker crumbs, cheddar cheese, eggs, bacon, red pimento, salt and black pepper to the onion. Stir until combined.

Preheat the oven to 350°. Lightly spray a 11 x 7 casserole dish with non stick cooking spray. Spoon the casserole into the dish. Sprinkle 3/4 cup cracker crumbs over the top. Bake for 45 minutes or until hot, bubbly and the casserole set. Remove from the oven and serve.

Squash Tomato Bake

Makes 8 servings

2 lbs. yellow squash, sliced
1 cup water
2 can stewed tomatoes, 14 oz. size
1 tbs. all purpose flour
2 tsp. granulated sugar
1 tsp. salt
1 tsp. paprika
1/2 tsp. garlic powder
1/4 tsp. black pepper
2 cups shredded mozzarella cheese
1/2 cup grated Parmesan cheese

Add the squash and water to a sauce pan over medium heat. Bring to a boil. Place a lid on the pan and reduce the heat to low. Simmer for 8 minutes or until the squash are tender. Remove the pan from the heat and drain all the liquid from the pan.

Drain the tomatoes but reserve 1/4 cup liquid. Add the tomatoes, 1/4 cup tomato liquid, all purpose flour, granulated sugar, salt, paprika, garlic powder and black pepper to a sauce pan over medium heat. Stir constantly and bring to a boil. Reduce the heat to low and simmer for 5 minutes. Remove the pan from the heat.

Preheat the oven to 350°. Lightly spray a 11 x 7 baking pan with non stick cooking spray. Spread half the squash in the bottom of the dish. Spread 1/4 of the tomato sauce over the squash. Sprinkle 1 cup mozzarella cheese over the sauce. Spread 1/4 of the tomato sauce over the cheese. Repeat the step one more time.

Sprinkle the Parmesan cheese over the top of the casserole. Bake for 30 minutes. Remove from the oven and cool for 10 minutes before serving.

Veggie Mac & Cheese Casserole

Makes 12 servings

1 1/2 cups dry elbow macaroni
3 cups fresh broccoli florets
2 cups fresh cauliflower florets
3 large carrots, halved and thinly sliced
2 celery ribs, sliced
1 cup chopped onion
1 tbs. unsalted butter
1/4 cup all purpose flour
1 cup whole milk
1 cup chicken broth
3 cups shredded sharp cheddar cheese
1 tbs. Dijon mustard
1/4 tsp. salt
1/8 tsp. black pepper
1/4 tsp. paprika

In a large sauce pan over medium heat, add 12 cups water. Bring the water to a boil and add the elbow macaroni. Cook for 4 minutes. Add the broccoli, cauliflower, carrots and celery to the pan. Cook for 6 minutes or until the macaroni and vegetables are tender. Remove the pan from the heat and drain all the water from the pan.

In a large skillet over medium heat, add the onion and butter. Saute for 5 minutes. Add the all purpose flour to the skillet. Stir constantly and cook for 2 minutes. Add the milk and chicken broth to the skillet. Stir constantly and cook about 5 minutes or until the sauce thickens and bubbles. Remove the skillet from the heat.

Add the cheddar cheese, Dijon mustard, salt and black pepper to the sauce. Stir until the cheese melts. Add the sauce to the macaroni and vegetables. Stir until combined. Spray a 9 x 13 baking pan with non stick cooking spray. Spoon the macaroni and cheese into the baking pan. Sprinkle the paprika over the top.

Preheat the oven to 350°. Bake for 20 minutes or until hot and bubbly. Remove the pan from the oven and serve.

Cauliflower Broccoli Bake

Makes 12 servings

5 cups cauliflower florets
4 cups broccoli florets
1 cup chopped onion
2 garlic cloves, minced
1 tbs. unsalted butter
2 cups chopped tomatoes
3/4 tsp. dried basil
3/4 tsp. dried oregano
3/4 tsp. salt
1/4 tsp. black pepper
1/4 tsp. Tabasco sauce
4 eggs
1/3 cup half and half cream
1 1/2 cups shredded Swiss cheese
1/4 cup shredded Parmesan cheese

In a sauce pan over medium heat, add the cauliflower and broccoli. Cover the vegetables with water and bring to a boil. Cook for 5 minutes or until the vegetables are crisp tender. Remove the pan from the heat and drain all the water from the pan.

In a large skillet over medium heat, add the onion, garlic and butter. Saute for 5 minutes. Add the tomatoes, basil, oregano, salt, black pepper, Tabasco sauce, broccoli and cauliflower. Stir until combined and thoroughly heated. Remove the skillet from the heat.

In a mixing bowl, add the eggs, cream, Swiss cheese and Parmesan cheese. Whisk until combined. Add the vegetables to the bowl. Stir until combined.

Preheat the oven to 375°. Spray a 2 quart casserole dish with non stick cooking spray. Spoon the casserole into the dish. Bake for 25 minutes or until a knife inserted in the center of the dish comes out clean. Remove from the oven and serve.

Polenta Corn Casserole

Makes 6 servings

14 oz. can vegetable broth
1/2 cup plain white or yellow cornmeal
8 oz. can whole kernel corn, drained
4 oz. can diced green chiles, drained
1/4 cup diced red bell pepper
1/2 tsp. salt
1/4 tsp. black pepper
1 cup shredded cheddar cheese

Add the vegetable broth to a 4 quart slow cooker. Whisk in the cornmeal. Add the corn, green chiles, red bell pepper, salt and black pepper to the slow cooker. Stir until combined. Set the temperature to low and cook for 4 hours or until the casserole thickens.

Add the cheddar cheese to the slow cooker. Stir until combined. Cook for 20 minutes or until the cheese melts.

Scalloped Tomato & Corn Casserole

Makes 4 servings

15 oz. can cream style corn
14 oz. can diced tomatoes
3/4 cup saltine cracker crumbs
1 beaten egg
2 tsp. granulated sugar
3/4 tsp. black pepper
1 cup chopped fresh tomatoes
1/4 cup chopped fresh parsley

Add the corn, canned tomatoes with juice, cracker crumbs, egg, granulated sugar and black pepper to a 4 quart slow cooker. Stir until combined. Set the temperature to low and cook for 4-6 hours or until bubbling hot and most of the liquid has evaporated.

Sprinkle the fresh tomatoes and parsley over the top before serving.

Glazed Broccoli with Almonds

Makes 6 servings

6 cups fresh broccoli spears
1/2 tsp. salt
1 1/2 cups hot water
1 beef bouillon cube
1 cup half and half
1/4 cup unsalted butter
1/4 cup all purpose flour
2 tbs. sherry
2 tbs. lemon juice
1/8 tsp. black pepper
1/2 cup shredded cheddar cheese
1/4 cup slivered almonds

In a sauce pan over medium heat, add the broccoli, salt and 3/4 cup water. Bring to a boil and cook for 5 minutes or until the broccoli is crisp tender. Remove the pan from the heat and drain all the water from the broccoli. Place the broccoli in a 12 x 8 x 2 casserole dish.

In a mixing bowl, add 3/4 cup hot water and the bouillon cube. Stir until the bouillon dissolves. Whisk in the half and half and set aside for the moment.

Preheat the oven to 375°. In a sauce pan over medium heat, add the butter. When the butter melts, add the all purpose flour. Stir constantly and cook for 1 minute. Slowly whisk in the bouillon mixture. Stir constantly and cook until the sauce thickens and bubbles. Remove the pan from the heat and stir in the sherry, lemon juice and black pepper.

Pour the sauce over the broccoli in the casserole dish. Sprinkle the cheddar cheese and almonds over the top of the dish. Bake for 25 minutes. Remove the dish from the oven and serve.

Creamy Parmesan Broccoli

Makes 5 servings

1 lb. pkg. frozen broccoli spears
2 tbs. olive oil
3/4 cup grated Parmesan cheese
1/2 cup chopped green onions
1/2 cup sour cream
1/4 cup mayonnaise
2 tbs. whole milk
1/8 tsp. black pepper
1/4 cup chopped toasted walnuts

Preheat the oven to 350°. In a sauce pan over medium heat, add the broccoli. Cover the broccoli with water and bring to a boil. Cook for 7 minutes or until the broccoli is crisp tender. Remove the pan from the heat and drain all the water from the pan.

Spread the broccoli in a 12 x 8 casserole dish. Drizzle the olive oil over the broccoli. Sprinkle 1/4 cup Parmesan cheese over the broccoli. Toss until the broccoli is coated in the oil and cheese.

In a mixing bowl, add 1/2 cup Parmesan cheese, green onions, sour cream, mayonnaise, milk and black pepper. Whisk until combined and spoon over the broccoli.

Bake for 18 minutes or until the sauce bubbles and is lightly browned. Remove from the oven and sprinkle the walnuts over the top.

Broccoli With Roasted Garlic & Tomatoes

Makes 4 servings

8 large garlic cloves
6 cups broccoli florets
2 tbs. olive oil
2 cups grape tomatoes
4 tbs. unsalted butter
1 1/2 tsp. salt
1 1/2 tsp. black pepper
6 tbs. grated Parmesan cheese

Place the garlic cloves on a large sheet of aluminum foil. Sprinkle 2 teaspoons water over the garlic. Close the foil around the garlic to form a packet and place on a baking sheet. Preheat the oven to 425°. Bake for 20 minutes or until the garlic is tender. Remove from the oven and cool for 10 minutes.

Squeeze the clove from the garlic into a bowl. Mash the garlic with a fork. Add the broccoli and olive oil to the bowl. Toss until well combined. Spray a large cast iron skillet with non stick cooking spray. Spread the broccoli in the skillet.

Increase the oven temperature to 450°. Bake for 10 minutes or until the broccoli begins to brown. Add the tomatoes, butter, salt and black pepper to the skillet. Stir until the butter melts and all the ingredients are combined. Bake for 10 minutes. Remove from the oven and sprinkle the Parmesan cheese over the top.

Kohlrabi Carrot Bake

Makes 6 servings

3 medium kohlrabies, peeled and sliced
4 carrots, sliced
1/4 cup chopped onion
3 tbs. unsalted butter
2 tbs. all purpose flour
1/2 tsp. salt
1/8 tsp. black pepper
1 1/2 cups whole milk
1/4 cup minced fresh parsley
1 tbs. lemon juice
3/4 cup soft breadcrumbs

Add the kohlrabies and carrots to a large sauce pan over medium heat. Cover the vegetables with water. Bring to a boil and reduce the heat to low. Place a lid on the pan. Cook for 15-20 minutes or until the vegetables are tender. Remove the pan from the heat and drain all the water from the pan.

In a skillet over medium heat, add the onion and 2 tablespoons butter. Saute for 4 minutes. Add the all purpose flour, salt and black pepper to the pan. Stir constantly for 2 minutes. Add the milk to the pan. Stir constantly and cook about 5 minutes or until the sauce thickens and bubbles. Remove the pan from the heat. Add the kohlrabies, carrots, parsley and lemon juice to the pan. Stir until combined.

Preheat the oven to 350°. Spray a 2 quart casserole dish with non stick cooking spray. Spoon the vegetables into the dish. In a small skillet over medium heat, add 1 tablespoon butter. When the butter melts, add the breadcrumbs. Stir constantly and cook about 3 minutes or until the breadcrumbs are toasted. Remove the skillet from the heat and sprinkle the breadcrumbs over the vegetables.

Bake for 25 minutes or until the dish is hot and bubbly. Remove from the oven and serve.

Spinach Cheese Casserole

Makes 8 servings

2 pkgs. thawed frozen chopped spinach, 10 oz. size
32 oz. carton cottage cheese
6 eggs
1/4 cup melted unsalted butter
8 oz. pkg. sharp American cheese slices, cut into bite size pieces
1/4 cup plus 2 tbs. all purpose flour
1/4 tsp. dried thyme

Drain the spinach and press the spinach with paper towels to remove all the moisture from the spinach. Preheat the oven to 350°. Spray a 9 x 13 casserole dish with non stick cooking spray. Add the spinach, cottage cheese, eggs, melted butter, American cheese, all purpose flour and thyme to the casserole dish. Stir until well combined.

Bake for 40 minutes or until the casserole is set and the cheeses melted. Remove the dish from the oven and cool for 5 minutes before serving.

Spinach Artichoke Bake

Makes 6 servings

2 pkgs. frozen chopped spinach, 10 oz. size
14 oz. can artichoke hearts, drained
1/2 cup finely chopped onion
1/4 cup unsalted butter, melted
1 cup sour cream
1/4 tsp. salt
1/4 tsp. black pepper
1/2 cup freshly grated Parmesan cheese

In a microwavable bowl, add the spinach. Cover the bowl with plastic wrap. Microwave for 5 minutes or until the spinach is thawed. Remove the bowl from the microwave and drain all the liquid from the spinach. Press the spinach with paper towels to remove the moisture.

Drain the artichokes hearts but save 1/4 cup liquid. Chop the artichoke hearts. In a skillet over medium heat, add the onion and butter. Saute for 4 minutes. Add the spinach, artichoke hearts, 1/4 cup artichoke liquid, sour cream, salt, black pepper and 1/4 cup Parmesan cheese. Stir until combined and remove the skillet from the heat.

Lightly spray a 1 1/2 quart casserole dish with non stick cooking spray. Spoon the casserole into the dish. Sprinkle 1/4 cup Parmesan cheese over the top of the casserole. Preheat the oven to 350°. Bake for 25 minutes or until hot and bubbly. Remove the dish from the oven and serve.

Baked Spinach Parmesan

Makes 4 servings

2 pkgs. fresh spinach, 10 oz. size
1/4 cup water
1/2 cup freshly grated Parmesan cheese
1/4 cup whipping cream
2 1/2 tbs. melted unsalted butter
3 tbs. finely chopped onion
1/8 tsp. black pepper
1/2 cup fresh breadcrumbs

Remove the stems from the spinach leaves and add the spinach and water to a large sauce pan over medium heat. Cook for 8 minutes or until the spinach is tender. Remove the pan from the heat and drain all the water from the pan. Pat the spinach dry with paper towels to remove the moisture.

Add the Parmesan cheese, whipping cream, butter, onion and black pepper to the spinach. Stir until combined. Lightly spray a 1 quart baking dish with non stick cooking spray. Spoon the spinach into the dish. Sprinkle the breadcrumbs over the top. Preheat the oven to 450°. Bake for 15 minutes or until hot and bubbly. Remove from the oven and serve.

Cheesy Swiss Spinach

Makes 6 servings

16 cups fresh spinach, washed and stems removed
1 tbs. half and half
1/8 tsp. salt
1/8 tsp. black pepper
1 large onion, chopped
2 tbs. unsalted butter
1 cup shredded Swiss cheese
3 large tomatoes, peeled and chopped

Tear the spinach into bite size pieces. In a dutch oven, add the spinach. Do not add water. Place a lid on the pan and place over high heat. Cook for 4 minutes. Remove the pan from the heat and drain all the liquid from the pan.

Add the half and half, salt, black pepper, onion and butter to the pan. Saute the spinach for 5 minutes. Remove the pan from the heat and stir in the Swiss cheese and tomatoes.

Spray a 2 quart casserole dish with non stick cooking spray. Spoon the spinach in the casserole dish. Turn the oven to the broiler position. Broil for 5 minutes. Remove the dish from the oven and serve.

Oyster and Spinach Casserole

Makes 4 servings

10 oz. pkg. frozen chopped spinach
1/4 cup water
1/2 pt. drained fresh oysters
1/4 cup grated Parmesan cheese
1/8 tsp. garlic powder
1/8 tsp. black pepper
3 slices bacon, cooked and crumbled
2 tbs. melted unsalted butter
1 tbs. lemon juice

In a sauce pan over medium heat, add the spinach and water. Bring the spinach to a boil and simmer for 5 minutes or until the spinach is tender. Remove the pan from the heat and drain all liquid from the spinach.

Spray a 1 quart casserole dish with non stick cooking spray. Preheat the oven to 450°. Add the spinach to the casserole dish. In a mixing bowl, add the oysters, Parmesan cheese, garlic powder, and black pepper. Stir until combined and spoon over the spinach.

Sprinkle the bacon over the top of the oysters. Drizzle the melted butter and lemon juice over the top of the dish. Bake for 7 minutes or until the oysters curl and the dish is hot and bubbly. Remove from the oven and serve.

Spinach Cheese Puff

Makes 6 servings

12 slices day old bread
2 cups shredded cheddar cheese
10 oz. pkg. frozen chopped spinach, thawed
1 cup cooked sliced mushrooms
4 eggs
2 1/2 cups whole milk
1 tbs. grated onion
1/2 tsp. yellow prepared mustard
1/4 tsp. salt
1/8 tsp. cayenne pepper
1/8 tsp. black pepper

Trim the crust from the bread. Spray a 9 x 13 baking dish with non stick cooking spray. Place 6 bread slices in the bottom of the baking dish. Sprinkle the cheddar cheese over the bread. Drain all liquid from the spinach. Press the spinach with paper towels if needed to remove the moisture.

Spoon the spinach and mushrooms over the cheese. In a mixing bowl, add the eggs, milk, onion, mustard, salt, cayenne pepper and black pepper. Whisk until well combined. Pour the egg mixture over the casserole. Cover the dish and refrigerate at least 6 hours but no longer than 12 hours.

Remove the casserole from the refrigerator and allow the casserole to sit for 45 minutes at room temperature. Preheat the oven to 325° Remove the cover from the casserole dish. Bake for 35-45 minutes or until the center is set, the dish puffed and golden brown. Remove from the oven and serve.

Smothered Kale

Makes 6 servings

12 cups chopped fresh kale
2 tbs. unsalted butter
2 tbs. all purpose flour
1 cup whole milk
1/2 tsp. salt
3 hard boiled eggs, chopped
1 cup shredded cheddar cheese

Remove the stems from the kale and wash the kale thoroughly. Tear the kale into bite size pieces. Add the kale to a large dutch oven. Do not add water to the pan. Place a lid on the pan and cook over high heat. Cook about 5 minutes or until the kale is wilted. Remove the pan from the heat and drain all the liquid from the kale.

In a sauce pan over medium heat, add the butter. When the butter melts, add the all purpose flour. Stir constantly and cook for 1 minute. Add the milk and salt to the pan. Stir constantly and cook until the sauce thickens. Remove the pan from the heat and stir in the eggs and kale.

Preheat the oven to 400°. Spray a 10 x 6 x 2 casserole dish with non stick cooking spray. Spread half the kale over the casserole dish. Sprinkle 1/2 cup cheddar cheese over the kale. Spread the remaining kale over the cheese and sprinkle 1/2 cup cheddar cheese over the top. Bake for 10-12 minutes or until the dish is bubbly and the cheese melted. Remove from the oven and serve.

Homestyle Broccoli Casserole

Makes 8 servings

2 beaten eggs
10.75 oz. can cream of mushroom soup
1 cup chopped onion
1 cup shredded cheddar cheese
1 cup shredded Swiss cheese
1/2 cup mayonnaise
2 tbs. melted unsalted butter
16 oz. pkg. frozen broccoli cuts, thawed
1/4 cup dry breadcrumbs

Preheat the oven to 400°. Spray a 1 1/2 quart casserole dish with non stick cooking spray. In a mixing bowl, add the eggs, cream of mushroom soup, onion, cheddar cheese, Swiss cheese, mayonnaise and butter. Stir until well combined.

Gently fold the broccoli into the sauce. Spoon the broccoli into the prepared dish. Sprinkle the breadcrumbs over the top. Bake for 30 minutes or until hot and bubbly. Remove the dish from the oven and serve.

Asparagus Artichoke Casserole

Makes 8 servings

1/2 cup chopped green bell pepper
1 tbs. melted unsalted butter
1 lb. pkg. frozen chopped asparagus, cooked
1/4 cup water
10.75 oz. can cream of mushroom soup
1 cup drained jarred artichoke hearts, chopped
1 1/2 cups sliced fresh mushrooms
1/3 cup chopped black olives
3 hard boiled eggs, chopped
1 1/4 cups shredded cheddar cheese

In a large skillet over medium heat, add the green bell pepper and butter. Saute for 4 minutes. Add the asparagus, water and cream of mushroom soup. Stir until combined and remove the skillet from the heat.

Preheat the oven to 350°. Place half the asparagus in the bottom of a 2 quart casserole dish. Place half the artichokes, mushrooms, black olives and eggs over the top of the asparagus. Repeat the layering process one more time. Bake for 30 minutes. Sprinkle the cheddar cheese over the top. Bake for 10 minutes. Remove the dish from the oven and serve.

Corn Stuffing Casserole

Makes 16 servings

12 oz. pkg. unseasoned stuffing cubes
1 onion, finely chopped
1/2 cup green bell pepper
1/2 cup red bell pepper
1/2 cup yellow bell pepper
1 tsp. garlic powder
1/2 tsp. salt
1/4 tsp. black pepper
3 beaten eggs
15 oz. can whole kernel corn, drained
15 oz. can cream style corn
1/2 cup melted unsalted butter
1 cup chicken broth

In a large mixing bowl, add the stuffing, onion, green bell pepper, red bell pepper, yellow bell pepper, garlic powder, salt, black pepper, eggs, whole kernel corn, cream style corn and butter. Toss until well combined. Add 1/2 cup chicken broth to the bowl. Stir until combined.

You may not use all the chicken broth. Add the remaining chicken broth as needed to make a moist but not soupy stuffing. Preheat the oven to 350°. Spray a 9 x 13 baking pan with non stick cooking spray. Spread the stuffing in the baking pan. Cover the pan with aluminum foil.

Bake for 30 minutes. Remove the aluminum foil from the pan. Bake for 15 minutes or until the stuffing is set and hot. Remove from the oven and serve.

Parmesan Onion Bake

Makes 6 servings

6 onions, peeled & diced
1 cup diced celery
8 tbs. unsalted butter
1/4 cup all purpose flour
1 tsp. salt
1/8 tsp. black pepper
1 1/2 cups whole milk
1/3 cup grated Parmesan cheese
1/2 cup chopped pecans

In a large skillet over medium heat, add the onion, celery and 3 tablespoons butter. Saute for 10 minutes. Remove the skillet from the heat and drain off any liquid.

In a sauce pan over medium heat, add 5 tablespoons butter. When the butter melts, add the all purpose flour, salt and black pepper. Stir constantly and cook for 2 minutes. Add the milk to the pan. Stir constantly and cook about 4 minutes or until the sauce thickens and bubbles. Remove the pan from the heat and spoon over the onions. Stir until combined.

Preheat the oven to 350°. Lightly spray a 2 quart baking dish with non stick cooking spray. Spoon the casserole into the dish. Sprinkle the Parmesan cheese and pecans over the top. Bake for 25 minutes or until hot and bubbly. Remove from the oven and serve.

4 SOUPS & SALADS

Green vegetables make wonderful salads. They are healthy, light and fill you up. Incorporate as many green salads into your menu plans as possible.

Soups are an easy way to get the family to eat more vegetables. Add your favorite sandwich or salad to a bowl of vegetable soup and you are ready to eat.

Picnic Vegetable Salad

I am asked to bring this salad to every barbecue and potluck. It is a crowd pleaser.

Makes 12-16 servings

4 tomatoes, cut into bite size pieces
2 cucumbers, cut into bite size pieces
2 cups yellow squash, cut into bite size pieces
1 onion, chopped
1/4 cup chopped fresh basil
2 tbs. chopped fresh parsley
1/2 cup vegetable oil
1/4 cup red wine vinegar
2 tbs. lemon juice
1 garlic clove, finely chopped
1 cup cubed Italian bread
1/4 cup grated Parmesan cheese
1/2 cup sliced black olives

In a large bowl, add the tomatoes, cucumbers, yellow squash and onion. In a pint jar with a lid, add the basil, parsley, vegetable oil, red wine vinegar, lemon juice and garlic. Place the lid on the jar and shake until combined.

Pour the dressing over the salad and toss until the vegetables are coated in the dressing. Cover the bowl and refrigerate at least 2 hours before serving. Toss again before serving.

When ready to serve, sprinkle the Italian bread, Parmesan cheese and olives over the top of the salad.

Garden Cabbage Salad

Makes 8 servings

3/4 cup mayonnaise
1/4 cup vinegar
1/4 cup granulated sugar
1 tsp. celery seeds
1/8 tsp. salt
1/8 tsp. black pepper
6 cups finely shredded cabbage
8 green onions, chopped
1 carrot, shredded
1 green bell pepper, finely chopped
1 cucumber, finely chopped
6 radishes, thinly sliced

In a mixing bowl, add the mayonnaise, vinegar, granulated sugar, celery seeds, salt and black pepper. Stir until combined. Add the cabbage, green onions, carrot, green bell pepper, cucumber and radishes to a large bowl.

Add the mayonnaise dressing to the salad and toss until combined. Chill before serving if desired.

Chinese Cabbage Salad

Makes 6 servings

1 large head Chinese cabbage, chopped
2 small purple onions, thinly sliced and separated into rings
1 cup sour cream
1/2 cup chopped onion
2 tbs. vinegar
2 tsp. celery seeds
1 tsp. salt
1/8 tsp. black pepper

Add the cabbage and onion to a large bowl. In a small bowl, add the sour cream, onion, vinegar, celery seeds, salt and black pepper. Whisk until combined. Pour the dressing over the cabbage and toss until combined.

Cover the bowl and chill at least 2 hours before serving.

Pickled Red Cabbage

Makes 6 servings

3 tbs. unsalted butter
6 cups finely shredded red cabbage
3/4 cup cranberry juice
2 tbs. vinegar
1/4 tsp. salt
1/4 cup granulated sugar

In a large skillet over low heat, add the butter. When the butter melts, add the cabbage. Stir frequently and cook about 4 minutes or until the cabbage is wilted.

Add the cranberry juice, vinegar and salt. Stir until well combined. Place a lid on the skillet. Reduce the heat to low and simmer the cabbage for 15 minutes. Stir in the granulated sugar and cook for 3 minutes. Remove the skillet from the heat. Serve warm or chilled.

Broccoli Salad

Makes 8 servings

1/2 cup sour cream
1/3 cup mayonnaise
3 tbs. apple cider vinegar
3/4 tsp. celery seeds
3/4 tsp. dry mustard
1/4 tsp. salt
1/8 tsp. black pepper
8 cups fresh broccoli florets, cut into bite size pieces
8 green onions, cut into thin slices
1 cup green pimento stuffed olives, sliced
8 oz. can sliced water chestnuts, drained

In a small bowl, add the sour cream, mayonnaise, apple cider vinegar, celery seeds, dry mustard, salt and black pepper. Stir until well combined.

In a large bowl, add the broccoli, green onions, olives and water chestnuts. Pour the dressing over the salad and toss until combined. Cover the bowl and chill for 1 hour before serving.

Creamy Broccoli Raisin Salad

Makes 8 servings

4 cups fresh broccoli florets
1/3 cup raisins
2 tbs. chopped onion
2 slices bacon, cooked and crumbled
3 oz. pkg. cream cheese, softened
2 tbs. granulated sugar
2 tbs. white vinegar
2 tbs. vegetable oil
1 tbs. yellow prepared mustard
1 garlic clove, minced

Cut the broccoli into bite size pieces. Add the broccoli, raisins, onion and half the bacon to a serving bowl. In a blender, add the cream cheese, granulated sugar, white vinegar, vegetable oil, mustard and garlic. Process until smooth and combined. Pour the dressing over the broccoli. Toss until well combined. Cover the bowl and chill for 3 hours. Sprinkle the remaining bacon over the top before serving.

Broccoli Corn Salad

Makes 8 servings

4 cups fresh broccoli florets
1 cup water
2 cups frozen whole kernel corn, thawed
1/2 cup chopped red bell pepper
1/4 cup plus 2 tbs. rice vinegar
3 tbs. vegetable oil
1/4 tsp. salt
1/8 tsp. black pepper
1/8 tsp. ground cumin
1/8 tsp. chili powder
1/8 tsp. dried oregano

Cut the broccoli into bite size pieces. In a sauce pan over medium heat, add the broccoli and water. Bring the broccoli to a boil and cook for 2 minutes. Add the whole kernel corn and cook for 4 minutes. Remove the pan from the heat and drain all the water from the vegetables. Rinse the vegetables in cold water and drain all the water again. Refrigerate the vegetables until chilled.

In a large bowl, add the broccoli, corn and red bell pepper. In a jar with a lid, add the rice vinegar, vegetable oil, salt, black pepper, cumin, chili powder and oregano. Place the lid on the jar and shake until well combined. Pour the dressing over the vegetables. Toss until well combined. Cover the bowl with a lid and chill for 2 hours before serving. Toss the salad again before serving.

Warm Broccoli Salad

Makes 6 servings

6 cups fresh broccoli florets
3 cups water
4 slices bacon
1/2 cup sliced green onions
1/4 cup balsamic vinegar
1 tsp. granulated sugar
1/2 tsp. salt
1/4 tsp. black pepper
8 oz. can sliced water chestnuts, drained
2 oz. jar diced red pimentos, drained
1 hard boiled egg, minced

In a large sauce pan over medium heat, add the broccoli and water. Bring the broccoli to a boil and cook for 3 minutes. Remove the pan from the heat and drain all the water from the pan. Rinse the broccoli in cold water and drain all the water again.

In a large skillet over medium heat, add the bacon. Cook about 7 minutes or until the bacon is crisp. Remove the bacon from the skillet and drain on paper towels. Leave the bacon drippings in the skillet. Crumble the bacon and set aside for the moment.

Add the green onions, balsamic vinegar, granulated sugar, salt and black pepper to the skillet. Stir constantly and cook until the sauce boils. Add the broccoli and red pimento to the skillet. Stir constantly and cook for 2 minutes. Remove the skillet from the heat and spoon the salad into a serving bowl. Sprinkle the bacon and egg over the top.

Barley Broccoli Salad

Makes 4 servings

1 cup water
1/2 tsp. salt
1/2 cup barley
1 cup chopped fresh broccoli florets
1/3 cup Italian dressing
1 1/4 cups chopped tomato
1/4 cup shredded carrot
2 tbs. diced onion
2 tbs. diced green bell pepper
2 oz. jar diced red pimentos
2 cups shredded lettuce

In a sauce pan over medium heat, add the water, salt and barley. Bring the barley to a boil and place a lid on the pan. Simmer about 15 minutes or until the barley is tender. Most of the water should be absorbed. Remove the pan from the heat and drain off any remaining liquid. Cool for 10 minutes.

In a mixing bowl, add the broccoli and Italian dressing. Toss until combined. Add the barley, tomato, carrot, onion, green bell pepper and red pimentos. Toss until combined. Cover the bowl and chill for 30 minutes.

Place the lettuce on 4 serving plates. Spoon the salad over the lettuce and serve.

Broccoli and Cauliflower Salad

Makes 8 servings

4 cups fresh cauliflower florets
4 cups fresh broccoli florets
2 cup sliced fresh mushrooms
1 cup thinly sliced celery
1 small purple onion, thinly sliced and separated into rings
1 cup vegetable oil
1/3 cup white wine vinegar
1/2 cup granulated sugar
1 tbs. dried Italian seasoning
2 tsp. dry mustard
1 tsp. salt

Add the cauliflower, broccoli, mushrooms, celery and purple onion to a large serving bowl. In a mixing bowl, add the vegetable oil, white wine vinegar, granulated sugar, Italian seasoning, dry mustard and salt. Whisk until well combined.

Pour the dressing over the vegetables in the bowl. Toss until well combined. Cover the bowl and chill for 3 hours before serving. Toss the salad again before serving. Drain the dressing from the salad before serving.

Crunchy Vegetable Salad

Makes 8 servings

6 cups fresh broccoli florets
3 cups fresh cauliflower florets
3 carrots, sliced
2 small zucchini, sliced
1 onion, thinly sliced and separated into rings
2/3 cup mayonnaise
1/3 cup vegetable oil
1/3 cup apple cider vinegar
1/4 cup granulated sugar
1 tbs. salt

Cut the broccoli and cauliflower into bite sized pieces. Add the broccoli, cauliflower, carrots, zucchini and onion to a large bowl. In a small bowl, whisk together the mayonnaise, vegetable oil, apple cider vinegar, granulated sugar and salt. Whisk until well combined.

Pour the mayonnaise dressing over the vegetables. Toss until the vegetables are coated with the dressing. Cover the bowl and chill for 6 hours before serving.

Zucchini Salad With Hot Bacon Dressing

Makes 6 servings

2 bacon slices
2 tbs. granulated sugar
2 tsp. cornstarch
1/3 cup cider vinegar
1/3 cup water
1 tsp. Worcestershire sauce
1/8 tsp. black pepper
4 cups shredded zucchini, patted dry
1/4 cup finely chopped onion
1 cup chopped fresh tomato
1 cup chopped fresh mushrooms

In a skillet over medium heat, add the bacon. Cook for 5 minutes or until the bacon is crisp. Remove the bacon from the skillet and drain on paper towels. Crumble the bacon.

Add the granulated sugar, cornstarch, cider vinegar, water, Worcestershire sauce and black pepper to the skillet. Stir constantly and bring to a boil. Cook for 1 minute or until the dressing thickens. Remove the skillet from the heat.

In a serving bowl, add the zucchini and onion. Pour the dressing over the zucchini. Toss until combined. Add the tomato and mushrooms to the bowl. Toss until combined and serve.

Honey Mustard Marinated Broccoli Salad

Makes 6 servings

3/4 cup prepared honey mustard salad dressing
1/3 cup white vinegar
1 tbs. poppy seeds
1/2 tsp. salt
4 cups fresh broccoli florets
1 cup fresh cauliflower florets
1 cup sliced fresh mushrooms
1/2 cup sliced onion
1/4 cup sliced celery

In a small bowl, add the honey mustard dressing, vinegar, poppy seeds and salt. Whisk until well combined. In a large bowl, add the broccoli, cauliflower, mushrooms, onion and celery. Pour the dressing over the vegetables and toss until combined.

Cover the bowl and chill for 3 hours. Toss the salad again before serving. You can drain off the dressing if desired before serving.

Grape Broccoli Salad

Makes 15 servings

6 cups fresh broccoli florets
6 green onions, sliced
1 cup diced celery
1 cup seedless green grapes
1 cup seedless red grapes
1 cup mayonnaise
1/3 cup granulated sugar
1 tbs. cider vinegar
8 oz. bacon, cooked and crumbled
1 cup toasted slivered almonds

In a large serving bowl, add the broccoli, green onions, celery, green grapes and red grapes. In a small bowl, add the mayonnaise, granulated sugar and cider vinegar. Whisk until combined and pour over the salad. Toss until combined.

Cover the bowl and refrigerate until chilled. When ready to serve, add the bacon and almonds. Toss until combined.

Overnight Green Vegetable Salad

Makes 10 servings

9 cups shredded iceberg lettuce
Salt and black pepper to taste
9 hard boiled eggs, diced
1 cup cooked chopped broccoli
1 1/2 lbs. cooked bacon, crumbled
3 cups shredded Swiss cheese
1 1/2 cups mayonnaise
1/2 cup sliced green onions

In a 3 quart bowl, add half the lettuce. Sprinkle the lettuce with salt and black pepper to taste. Place the hard boiled eggs over the lettuce. Sprinkle the eggs with salt and black pepper if desired.

Sprinkle the broccoli and the remaining lettuce over the eggs. Sprinkle the bacon and Swiss cheese over the top. Spread the mayonnaise over the top of the salad. Spread the mayonnaise to the edges of the bowl to seal in the salad. Sprinkle the green onions over the top.

Cover the bowl with a lid or plastic wrap. Refrigerate for 24 hours before serving.

Traditional Greek Salad

Makes 12 servings

1 head iceberg lettuce, torn into bite size pieces
2 cucumbers, sliced
3 tomatoes, cut into wedges
4 oz. can sliced black olives, drained
2 green onions, chopped
8 oz. crumbled feta cheese
1/4 cup olive oil
3 tbs. red wine vinegar
1 tsp. dried oregano
1/2 tsp. salt
1/8 tsp. black pepper

In a large salad bowl, add the lettuce, cucumbers, tomatoes, black olives, green onions and feta cheese. Toss until combined. In a small bowl, add the olive oil, red wine vinegar, oregano, salt and black pepper. Whisk until combined and pour over the salad. Toss until combined and serve.

Sesame Citrus Green Salad

Makes 4 servings

1 garlic clove, peeled
2 cups Boston lettuce
2 cups romaine lettuce
6 Belgian endive leaves
1 cup fresh grapefruit sections
1/2 cup fresh orange sections
1 tbs. toasted sesame seeds
2 tbs. vegetable oil
1 tbs. tarragon vinegar

Rub the garlic clove over the sides and bottom of a serving bowl. Discard the garlic clove. Add the Boston lettuce, romaine lettuce and endive leaves to the bowl. Cover the bowl and chill for 1 hour.

When the salad is chilled, place the grapefruit and orange sections over the lettuce. Sprinkle the sesame seeds over the top of the salad. In a small bowl, add the vegetable oil and tarragon vinegar. Whisk until well combined. Pour the dressing over the salad and toss until combined.

Marinated Mozzarella Green Salad

Makes 6 servings

1/2 cup olive oil
1/4 cup red wine vinegar
1 garlic clove, minced
1 tsp. dried thyme
1/2 tsp. salt
1/4 tsp. black pepper
8 oz. pkg. mozzarella cheese, cubed
4 cups mixed salad greens
4 green onions, sliced
2 tomatoes, cut into wedges
1 cucumber, sliced
1 red bell pepper, cut into thin strips
1/2 cup chopped fresh basil

In a 1 quart jar, add the olive, oil, red wine vinegar, garlic, thyme, salt and black pepper. Place the lid on the jar and shake until well combined. Add the mozzarella cubes and shake until the mozzarella cubes are coated in the dressing. Place the lid on the jar and refrigerate the cheese for 8 hours.

When ready to serve, add the mixed salad greens, green onions, tomatoes, cucumber, red bell pepper and basil to a large serving bowl. Pour the dressing and mozzarella cheese over the salad. Toss until combined and serve.

For an easy appetizer, drain the dressing off the mozzarella cubes and serve the cheese for a bite size appetizer. The cheese is also delicious on pizza or pasta.

Sesame Broccoli Cauliflower Salad

Makes 10 servings

3 cups fresh broccoli florets
3 cups fresh cauliflower florets
1/2 cup shredded carrot
1 tbs. rice vinegar
1/2 tsp. dark sesame oil
1 tsp. grated fresh ginger
1/2 tsp. salt
1/8 tsp. black pepper
1 garlic clove, minced
3 tbs. olive oil
2 tbs. toasted sesame seeds

Add the broccoli and cauliflower to a large sauce pan over medium heat. Cover the vegetables with water and bring to a boil. Boil for 2 minutes. Remove the pan from the heat and drain all the water from the pan. Rinse the vegetables with cold water until chilled.

Add the cauliflower, broccoli and carrot to a serving bowl. In a small bowl, add the rice vinegar, sesame oil, ginger, salt, black pepper and garlic. Whisk until combined. Continue whisking and slowly add the olive oil. Whisk until well combined and pour over the salad. Sprinkle the sesame seeds over the salad. Toss until the vegetables are coated in the dressing. Cover the bowl and refrigerate at least 2 hours before serving.

Island Paradise Salad

Makes 8 servings

1 tsp. grated lime zest
3 tbs. honey
2 tbs. fresh lime juice
1 tbs. vegetable oil
2 cups frozen sugar snap peas
3 cups torn romaine lettuce
3 cups torn Bibb lettuce
1 avocado, peeled, pitted and cut into 1/2" cubes
1 large mango, peeled, pitted and cut into 1/2" cubes
1 cup purple onion, separated into rings
1/2 cup unsweetened shredded coconut

In a small bowl, add the lime zest, honey, lime juice and vegetable oil. Whisk until well combined. Add the sugar snap peas to a sauce pan over medium heat. Add about 1/4 cup water to the peas. Bring to a boil and cook for 4 minutes or until the peas are tender. Remove the pan from the heat and drain all the water from the peas. Rinse the peas in cold water until chilled. Pat dry with paper towels.

In a serving bowl, add the sugar snap peas, romaine lettuce, Bibb lettuce, avocado, mango and purple onion. Toss until combined. Pour the dressing over the salad. Toss until the salad is coated in the dressing. Sprinkle the coconut over the top and serve.

Beet Green Salad

Makes 4 servings

1/4 cup olive oil
2 tbs. red wine vinegar
1 tbs. Dijon mustard
1 tbs. honey
1/4 tsp. salt
1/8 tsp. black pepper
1/8 tsp. ground nutmeg
3 cups curly endive
3 cups escarole, torn into bite size pieces
16 oz. can sliced beets, drained and diced

In a jar with a lid, add the olive oil, red wine vinegar, Dijon mustard, honey, salt, black pepper and ground nutmeg. Place the lid on the jar and shake until well combined.

Place the endive and escarole in a serving bowl. Pour the dressing over the greens and toss until combined. Spoon the beets over the top of the salad before serving.

Autumn Tossed Salad

Makes 10 servings

1/2 cup lemon juice
1/2 cup granulated sugar
2 tsp. finely chopped onion
1 tsp. Dijon mustard
1/2 tsp. salt
2/3 cup vegetable oil
1 tbs. poppy seeds
1 large head romaine lettuce, torn into bite size pieces
1 cup shredded Swiss cheese
1 cup unsalted cashews
1 apple, cored and chopped
1 pear, cored and chopped
1/4 cup dried cranberries

In a blender, add the lemon juice, granulated sugar, onion, Dijon mustard and salt. Process until combined. With the blender running, slowly add the vegetable oil. Blend until well combined. Spoon the dressing into a small bowl. Add the poppy seeds and stir until combined. Cover the bowl and refrigerate until well chilled.

In a serving bowl, add the lettuce, Swiss cheese, cashews, apple, pear and cranberries. Drizzle the dressing over the salad. Toss until combined and serve.

Spinach Rice Salad

Makes 6 servings

1/2 cup Italian salad dressing
1 tbs. soy sauce
1/2 tsp. granulated sugar
3 cups cooked long grain rice
2 cups shredded fresh spinach
1/2 cup sliced celery
1/2 cup sliced green onions
6 slices bacon, cooked and crumbled

In a large bowl, add the Italian salad dressing, soy sauce and granulated sugar. Whisk until well combined. Add the rice and stir until combined. Cover the bowl and chill for 2 hours.

When ready to serve, add the spinach, celery and green onions to the salad. Toss until combined. Sprinkle the bacon over the top.

Tossed Salad With Lemon Vinaigrette

Makes 10 servings

1/2 head fresh romaine lettuce
1/2 head iceberg lettuce
5 bacon slices, cooked and crumbled
1 cup cherry tomatoes, halved
1/2 cup slivered almonds
1/2 cup shredded Parmesan cheese
1/2 cup croutons
1 1/2 tbs. lemon juice
1 1/2 tbs. grated Parmesan cheese
1 garlic clove, minced
1/4 tsp. salt
1/8 tsp. black pepper
1/3 cup olive oil

Tear the romaine and iceberg lettuce into bite size pieces and add to a serving bowl. Add the bacon, cherry tomatoes, almonds, shredded Parmesan cheese and croutons to the bowl.

In a small bowl, add the lemon juice, grated Parmesan cheese, garlic, salt and black pepper. Whisk constantly and slowly add the olive oil. Whisk until well combined and pour over the salad. Toss until combined and serve.

Goat Cheese & Greens

Makes 6 servings

1/2 cup herb seasoned breadcrumbs
11 oz. log goat cheese, cut into 12 slices
Vegetable cooking spray
1/3 cup olive oil
3 tbs. lemon juice
1 tsp. dried basil
1/4 tsp. salt
1/8 tsp. black pepper
3 cups radicchio, torn into bite size pieces
6 cups arugula, torn into bite size pieces

Place the breadcrumbs in a shallow bowl. Dredge the goat cheese slices in the breadcrumbs. Preheat the oven to 400°. Spray the goat cheese slices with the vegetable cooking spray. Spray a baking sheet with vegetable cooking spray. Place the goat cheese slices on the baking sheet. Bake for 7 minutes or until the slices are golden brown. Remove from the oven.

In a jar with a lid, add the olive oil, lemon juice, basil, salt and black pepper. Place the lid on the jar and shake until well combined. Add the radicchio and arugula to a serving bowl. Pour the dressing over the greens and toss until combined. Place the goat cheese slices over the top of the salad and serve.

Tricolor Blue Cheese Salad

Makes 8 servings

2/3 cup olive oil
1/2 cup crumbled blue cheese
3 tbs. white wine vinegar
1 tsp. dried oregano
1/4 tsp. salt
1/4 tsp. black pepper
4 cups radicchio, torn into bite size pieces
4 cups arugula, torn into bite size pieces
8 cups Belgian endive, torn into bite size pieces

In a jar with a lid, add the olive oil, blue cheese, white wine vinegar, oregano, salt and black pepper. Place the lid on the jar and shake until well combined.

Add the radicchio, arugula and endive to a serving bowl. Add the dressing and toss until combined.

Tropical Spinach Salad

Makes 8 servings

1/4 cup granulated sugar
1/4 cup white vinegar
1/4 tsp. salt
1/4 tsp. dry mustard
1/4 tsp. dried minced onion
1/8 tsp. paprika
1 egg, beaten
1/4 cup vegetable oil
5 cups fresh spinach, torn into bite size pieces
3 cups romaine lettuce, torn into bite size pieces
2 cups leaf lettuce, torn into bite size pieces
11 oz. can mandarin oranges, drained
1 small purple onion, thinly sliced and separated into rings
1/4 cup toasted sliced almonds

In a small sauce pan over low heat, add the granulated sugar, white vinegar, salt, dry mustard, onion, paprika and egg. Whisk until well combined. Bring the dressing to a boil and remove the pan from the heat. Whisk constantly and slowly add the vegetable oil. Refrigerate the dressing until chilled.

In a large serving bowl, add the spinach, romaine lettuce, leaf lettuce, mandarin oranges and purple onion. Pour the chilled dressing over the greens. Toss until combined. Sprinkle the almonds over the top and serve.

Cranberry Spinach Salad

Makes 4 servings

1/3 cup olive oil
3 tbs. granulated sugar
2 tbs. white wine vinegar
2 tbs. sour cream
6 oz. fresh baby spinach
1/2 cup toasted walnuts
1/2 cup dried cranberries

In a glass jar, add the olive oil, granulated sugar, white wine vinegar and sour cream. Place the lid on the jar and shake until well combined. Add the spinach, walnuts and cranberries to a serving bowl. Drizzle the dressing over the salad. Toss until combined and serve.

Pecan Pear Spinach Salad

Makes 4 servings

6 cups fresh baby spinach
1 large pear, cored and thinly sliced
2/3 cup chopped toasted pecans
1/2 cup dried cherries
1/2 cup crumbled blue cheese
2 tbs. balsamic vinegar
1 tbs. soy sauce
1 tbs. honey
1 1/2 tsp. stone ground mustard
1 garlic clove, minced
1/4 tsp. salt
1/8 tsp. black pepper
1/2 cup olive oil

In a serving bowl, add the spinach, pear, pecans, cherries and blue cheese. Toss until combined. In a small bowl, add the balsamic vinegar, soy sauce, honey, mustard, garlic, salt and black pepper. Whisk until well combined. Whisk constantly and slowly add the olive oil. Whisk until well combined.

Pour the dressing over the salad. Toss until combined and serve.

Layered Spinach Salad

Makes 10 servings

1 lb. fresh spinach, torn into bite size pieces
Salt and black pepper to taste
1 lb. cooked bacon, crumbled
6 hard boiled eggs, chopped
10 oz. pkg. frozen green peas, thawed
1 onion, minced
1 cup sliced celery
1 cup mayonnaise
1/2 cup shredded cheddar cheese

Add the spinach to a large bowl. Season the spinach with salt and black pepper if desired. Sprinkle the bacon, eggs, green peas, onion and celery over the spinach. Spread the mayonnaise over the top of the salad. Sprinkle the cheddar cheese over the top.

Cover the bowl and chill for 2 hours before serving or serve at room temperature.

Spinach and Onion Salad Bowl

Makes 8 servings

3 tbs. cider vinegar
1 tbs. granulated sugar
1/2 tsp. salt
1/4 tsp. dry mustard
1/3 cup vegetable oil
3 large oranges
1 purple onion, thinly sliced and separated into rings
8 cups fresh spinach, torn into bite size pieces
6 bacon slices, cooked and crumbled

In a blender, add the cider vinegar, granulated sugar, salt, dry mustard and vegetable oil. Process until smooth and combined.

Peel the oranges and cut into sections. Add the oranges, onion rings and spinach to a large bowl. Pour the dressing over the salad. Toss until combined. Sprinkle the bacon crumbles over the top and serve.

Crunchy Spinach Cabbage Salad

Makes 6 servings

1/4 cup granulated sugar
3/4 tsp. dry mustard
3/4 tsp. salt
1/2 tsp. celery seeds
1 1/2 tbs. minced onion
1/4 cup vinegar
1/2 cup vegetable oil
6 cups fresh spinach, torn into bite size pieces
2 tbs. toasted slivered almonds
3/4 cup shredded purple cabbage
1/4 cup raisins

In a jar with a lid, add the granulated sugar, dry mustard, salt, celery seeds, minced onion, vinegar and vegetable oil. Place the lid on the jar and shake until combined.

In a large bowl, add the spinach, almonds, cabbage and raisins. Pour the dressing over the salad. Toss until well combined and serve.

Festive Spinach Salad

Makes 8 servings

3/4 cup granulated sugar
1/2 cup vinegar
1 cup vegetable oil
1 tsp. celery seeds
1 tsp. paprika
3/4 tsp. salt
16 cups fresh spinach, torn into bite size pieces
4 cups cauliflower florets, cut into bite size pieces
4 oz. jar diced red pimentos, drained
1 onion, thinly sliced
6 slices cooked bacon, crumbled

In a sauce pan over medium heat, add the granulated sugar and vinegar. Stir constantly and bring the dressing to a boil. Remove from the heat and whisk in the vegetable oil, celery seeds, paprika and salt. Place the dressing in the refrigerator for 3 hours.

Remove the dressing from the refrigerator and stir until well combined. In a large bowl, add the spinach, cauliflower, red pimentos and onion. Pour the dressing over the vegetables. Toss until combined. Sprinkle the bacon over the top and serve.

Sesame Spinach Salad

Makes 4 servings

1/4 cup vegetable oil
2 tbs. white wine vinegar
2 tbs. chopped fresh parsley
1 tsp. Beau Monde seasoning
1/4 tsp. salt
1/4 tsp. black pepper
1/4 tsp. dried savory
8 cups fresh spinach, torn into bite size pieces
1 tbs. toasted sesame seeds
1 cup seasoned croutons

In a small bowl, add the vegetable oil, white wine vinegar, parsley, Beau Monde seasoning, salt, black pepper and savory. Stir until well combined.

Add the spinach to a serving bowl. Add the dressing and toss until combined. Sprinkle the sesame seeds and croutons over the top.

Southern Spinach Salad

Makes 6 servings

3 tbs. vegetable oil
2 tbs. tarragon vinegar
1 tsp. granulated sugar
1/2 tsp. salt
1/2 tsp. ground ginger
1/8 tsp. paprika
6 cups torn fresh spinach
2 cups shredded iceberg lettuce
2 oranges, peeled and cut into sections
2 grapefruit, peeled and cut into sections

In a jar with a lid, add the vegetable oil, tarragon vinegar, granulated sugar, salt, ginger and paprika. Place the lid on the jar and shake until well combined.

In a large bowl, add the spinach, lettuce, oranges, grapefruit and dressing. Toss until combined and serve.

Asparagus Vinaigrette Salad

Makes 6 servings

3 cups fresh asparagus, trimmed and cut into 1" pieces
3/4 cup olive oil
1/4 cup vinegar
2 tbs. Dijon mustard
2 tbs. minced shallots
2 tbs. minced fresh parsley
1 tbs. chopped fresh chives
1 1/2 tsp. chopped fresh tarragon
2 hard boiled eggs, chopped

Add the asparagus to a sauce pan over medium heat. Cover the asparagus with water and bring to a boil. Simmer about 7 minutes or until the asparagus is crisp tender. Remove the pan from the heat and drain all the water from the asparagus. Rinse the asparagus in cold water and drain all the water again.

Place the asparagus in a serving dish. In a mixing bowl, add the olive oil, vinegar, Dijon mustard, shallots, parsley, chives and tarragon. Whisk until well combined. Pour the dressing over the asparagus. Cover the dish and chill before serving. When ready to serve, sprinkle the hard boiled eggs over the top.

Asparagus Fennel Pasta Salad

Makes 14 servings

1 lb. fresh asparagus, trimmed and cut into 3/4" pieces
2 onions, peeled, halved and thinly sliced
2 small fennel bulbs, sliced
1/4 cup plus 2 tbs. olive oil
8 oz. dry penne pasta
4 cups diced fresh tomatoes
12 pitted Greek olives, sliced
1 cup minced fresh parsley
1/4 cup lemon juice
2 garlic cloves, minced
1/2 tsp. Dijon mustard
1/2 tsp. salt
1/4 tsp. black pepper
1 cup crumbled feta cheese

Preheat the oven to 400°. Place the asparagus, onions and fennel slices on a large baking sheet. Drizzle 2 tablespoons olive oil over the vegetables. Toss until the vegetables are coated in the oil. Stir occasionally and bake for 20 minutes or until the vegetables are crisp tender and lightly browned. Remove the pan from the oven.

In a large sauce pan over medium heat, add 12 cups water. Bring the water to a boil and add the pasta. Cook about 8 minutes or until the pasta is tender. Remove the pan from the heat and drain all the water from the pasta.

Add the pasta, roasted vegetables, tomatoes, olive and parsley to a large serving bowl. In a small bowl, add the lemon juice, 1/4 cup olive oil, garlic, Dijon mustard, salt and black pepper. Whisk until well combined and pour over the salad. Toss until combined. Sprinkle the feta cheese over the top and serve.

Asparagus Potato Salad

Makes 8 servings

6 cups fresh asparagus
1 lb. small new potatoes
Water
1/4 cup white wine vinegar
1/4 cup diced purple onion
1 1/2 tsp. Dijon mustard
1/2 tsp. dried dill
1/4 tsp. black pepper
1 hard boiled egg, sliced

Trim the woody ends off the asparagus and remove the tough outer scales. Cut the asparagus into bite size pieces. In a sauce pan over medium heat, add the asparagus. Cover with water and cook about 10 minutes or until the asparagus is tender. Remove the pan from the heat and drain all the water from the pan. Rinse the asparagus with cold water and drain again. Cool the asparagus completely before using.

In a sauce pan over medium heat, add the new potatoes. Cover with water and bring to a boil. Cook about 7 minutes or until the potatoes are tender. Remove the pan from the heat and drain all the water from the potatoes. Rinse the potatoes with cold water and drain again. Cool the potatoes completely and cut into thin slices.

In a large bowl, add the asparagus and potatoes. In a small bowl, whisk together 1/4 cup water, white wine vinegar, purple onion, Dijon mustard, dill and black pepper. Pour the dressing over the potatoes and asparagus. Gently toss until combined. Cover the bowl and refrigerate for 3 hours. Toss the salad again before serving. Place the sliced egg over the top of the salad before serving.

Fresh Asparagus Tomato Salad

You can serve this delicious dish as a salad or a side dish. It makes a wonderful light lunch in the summertime. This is an easy dish for picnics or barbecue's.

Makes 12 servings

2 lbs. fresh asparagus spears
6 cups water
6 tomatoes, thinly sliced
1/3 cup shredded mozzarella cheese
3 tbs. chopped fresh basil
4 tbs. balsamic vinegar
Salt and black pepper to taste

Trim the woody ends from the asparagus. Peel the tough outer scales from the asparagus. In a large sauce pan over medium heat, add the water. Bring the water to a boil and add the asparagus spears. Cook for 6 minutes or until the asparagus is crisp tender. Remove the pan from the heat and drain all the water from the asparagus. Run cold water over the asparagus until chilled. Drain all the water from the asparagus.

On a serving platter, place the asparagus spears in the center of the platter. Arrange the tomato slices around the asparagus. Sprinkle the mozzarella cheese and basil over the tomatoes. Drizzle the balsamic vinegar over the tomatoes. Season with salt and black pepper.

Roasted Asparagus Salad

Makes 8 servings

1 1/2 lbs. fresh asparagus
1/2 cup olive oil
1 1/2 tbs. chopped fresh basil
1/2 tsp. lemon pepper
1/2 tsp. salt
1/4 cup balsamic vinegar
1 garlic clove, minced
1 cup cherry tomatoes, halved
1/2 cup chopped red bell pepper
1/4 cup finely chopped purple onion
1 head Bibb lettuce, torn into bite size pieces
1 avocado, sliced

Preheat the oven to 425°. Trim the scales and woody ends from the asparagus. In a mixing bowl, add 1 tablespoon olive oil, 1 1/2 teaspoons basil, lemon pepper and 1/4 teaspoon salt. Whisk until combined. Add the asparagus to the bowl. Toss until the asparagus are coated in the oil and seasonings.

Lightly spray a large baking sheet with non stick cooking spray. Spread the asparagus on the baking sheet. Bake for 15 minutes or until the asparagus is tender. Remove from the oven.

Add 1 tablespoon balsamic vinegar to a mixing bowl. In a small bowl, add the remaining balsamic vinegar, garlic, 1/4 teaspoon salt and the remaining olive oil. Whisk until combined. Add the tomatoes, red bell pepper and onion to the bowl with 1 tablespoon balsamic vinegar. Toss until combined. Add the asparagus and toss until combined.

Place the lettuce on a serving platter. Spoon the vegetables over the top of the lettuce. Sprinkle the remaining basil over the top. Spoon the avocado slices over the top and serve. Drizzle the dressing over the top and serve.

Asparagus Vegetable Salad

Makes 6 servings

1 lb. fresh asparagus, trimmed & cut into 1" pieces
1 small zucchini, halved and diced
1 cup cherry tomatoes
1/4 cup sliced green onions
1/4 cup minced fresh parsley
3 tbs. olive oil
2 tbs. red wine vinegar
1 garlic clove, minced
1/4 tsp. seasoned salt
1/4 tsp. Dijon mustard
1/4 cup shredded Parmesan cheese
2 tbs. toasted sunflower kernels

Add the asparagus and zucchini to a steamer basket. Place the basket in a sauce pan with 1" of water. Place the pan on the stove over medium heat. Place a lid on the pan and bring to a boil. Steam for 2 minutes. Remove the pan from the heat and rinse the asparagus and zucchini in cold water. Pat the vegetables dry with paper towels.

In a large bowl, add the asparagus, zucchini, cherry tomatoes, green onions and parsley. Toss until combined. In a small bowl, add the olive oil, red wine vinegar, garlic, seasoned salt and Dijon mustard. Whisk until combined and pour over the salad. Toss until combined. Sprinkle the Parmesan cheese and sunflower kernels over the top and serve.

Summer Vegetable Salad With Dill Dressing

Makes 6 servings

1 cup fresh cauliflower florets
1 cup fresh baby carrots
1 cup sliced purple onion
1 cup grape tomatoes, halved
1 cup chopped fresh zucchini
3 tbs. cider vinegar
2 tbs. olive oil
1 tsp. dried dill
1/2 tsp. salt
1/2 tsp. ground mustard
1/4 tsp. garlic powder
1/4 tsp. black pepper

In a serving bowl, add the cauliflower, carrots, onion, tomatoes and zucchini. In a small bowl, add the cider vinegar, olive oil, dill, salt, ground mustard, garlic powder and black pepper. Whisk until combined and pour over the salad. Toss until combined.

Cover the bowl and refrigerate at least 2 hours before serving. Drain off the dressing before serving.

Cucumber Salad

Makes 8 servings

7 cups thinly sliced peeled cucumbers
2 cups granulated sugar
1 large onion, peeled and chopped
1 green bell pepper, chopped
1 cup cider vinegar
1 tbs. salt
1 tbs. celery seed

Add all the ingredients to a serving bowl. Toss until combined. Cover the bowl and refrigerate at least 2 hours before serving. Drain the liquid from the salad before serving.

Roasted Onion Salad

Makes 8 servings

3 large onions, cut into 1/2" slices
1/4 cup plus 1/2 tsp. olive oil
4 garlic cloves
8 cups mixed salad greens, torn
1 cup crumbled blue cheese
1/2 cup toasted walnuts, chopped
2 tbs. white wine vinegar
2 shallots, quartered
1/4 cup minced fresh parsley
1/2 tsp. crushed red pepper flakes
2/3 cup olive oil

Preheat the oven to 400°. Spread the onions on a 15 x 10 x 1 baking sheet. Drizzle 1/4 cup olive oil over the onions. Toss until the onions are coated in the olive oil. Place the garlic cloves on a small sheet of aluminum foil. Drizzle 1/2 teaspoon olive oil over the garlic cloves. Fold the aluminum foil around the garlic. Place the garlic on the baking pan with the onions.

Bake for 45 minutes or until the onions are golden brown. Stir the onions occasionally while baking. Remove the pan from the oven and cool for 15 minutes.

In a large bowl, add the salad greens, blue cheese, walnuts and onions. Toss until combined. Add the white wine vinegar and shallots to a blender. Squeeze the garlic from the cloves into the blender. Pulse until well blended. Add the parsley and red pepper flakes to the blender. Pulse until combined. With the blender running, slowly add 2/3 cup olive oil. Blend until well combined. Serve the dressing with the salad.

Tomato Cucumber Mozzarella Salad

Makes 8 servings

1/3 cup olive oil
2 tbs. red wine vinegar
2 tbs. balsamic vinegar
1 tsp. granulated sugar
1/2 tsp. salt
1/2 tsp. dried oregano
1/4 tsp. black pepper
3 cups chopped fresh tomatoes
1 English cucumber, diced
1/2 cup chopped green bell pepper
1/4 cup thinly sliced onion
12 pitted Greek olives, sliced
2 tbs. minced fresh parsley
1 tbs. minced fresh basil
4 oz. fresh mozzarella cheese, cubed

In a glass jar, add the olive oil, red wine vinegar, balsamic vinegar, granulated sugar, salt, oregano and black pepper. Place the jar on the lid and shake until well combined.

In a large serving bowl, add the tomatoes, cucumber, green bell pepper, onion, olives, parsley and basil. Pour the dressing over the salad. Toss until combined. Sprinkle the mozzarella cheese over the top and serve.

Creamy Corn Salad

Makes 12 servings

6 cups frozen whole kernel corn, thawed
3 cups chopped fresh tomatoes
1 cup cubed avocado
2/3 cup julienned red bell pepper
2/3 cup julienned green bell pepper
1/2 cup chopped onion
1 cup mayonnaise
2 tbs. red wine vinegar
2 tbs. Dijon mustard
1 tsp. salt
1/8 tsp. black pepper

In a serving bowl, add the corn, tomatoes, avocado, red bell pepper, green bell pepper and onion. Toss until combined. In a small bowl, add the mayonnaise, red wine vinegar, Dijon mustard, salt and black pepper. Stir until combined and pour over the salad. Toss until combined. Cover the bowl and refrigerate about 1 hour or until chilled.

Green Bean and Tomato Salad

Makes 10 servings

12 cups fresh green beans
6 cups water
4 large tomatoes, cut into wedges
3/4 cup olive oil
1/4 cup plus 2 tbs. Worcestershire sauce
1/2 tsp. black pepper
Salt to taste
9 green onions, thinly sliced

Wash the green beans and trim the ends. Add the water to a large sauce pan over medium heat. Bring the water to a boil and add the green beans. Cook for 12 minutes or until the green beans are crisp tender. Remove the pan from the heat and drain all the water from the green beans. Rinse the beans with cold water and drain all the water again.

Add the green beans and tomatoes to a large bowl. In a jar with a lid, add the olive oil, Worcestershire sauce and black pepper. Place a lid on the jar and shake until combined. Season the dressing with salt to taste. Pour the dressing over the tomatoes and green beans. Toss until the vegetables are coated in the dressing. Cover the bowl and refrigerate for 3 hours.

When ready to serve, remove the green beans and tomatoes from the bowl. Place the vegetables on a platter. Sprinkle the green onions over the top.

Corn Lettuce Salad

Makes 4 servings

3 cups shredded lettuce
3/4 cup frozen whole kernel corn, thawed
2 tbs. granulated sugar
2 tbs. cider vinegar
1 1/2 tsp. poppy seeds
1/2 tsp. grated onion
1/4 tsp. salt
1/4 tsp. ground mustard
1/4 cup vegetable oil
1/4 cup finely chopped red bell pepper

In a serving bowl, add the lettuce and corn. Toss until combined. In a small bowl, add the granulated sugar, cider vinegar, poppy seeds, onion, salt, ground mustard, vegetable oil and red bell pepper. Whisk until combined and pour over the salad. Toss until combined and serve.

White Corn Salad

Makes 8 servings

2 tbs. olive oil
2 tbs. rice vinegar
1 tsp. light brown sugar
1/4 tsp. salt
1/8 tsp. black pepper
2 cans drained white shoe peg corn, 11 oz. size
1 1/2 cups chopped tomato
3 green onions, chopped
1/2 cup chopped green bell pepper

In a serving bowl, add the olive oil, rice vinegar, brown sugar, salt and black pepper. Whisk until well combined. Add the corn, tomato, green onions and green bell pepper to the bowl. Toss until combined. Cover the bowl and refrigerate at least 1 hour before serving.

Tomato Corn Salad

Makes 7 servings

3 cups chopped fresh tomatoes
1/2 cup purple onion, chopped
1/3 cup chopped green onion
1/4 cup balsamic vinegar
3 tbs. minced fresh basil
1 tbs. minced fresh cilantro
1 tsp. salt
1/2 tsp. black pepper
4 cups fresh corn kernels
3 garlic cloves, peeled and thinly sliced
2 tbs. olive oil
1 tbs. Dijon mustard

In a large bowl, add the tomatoes, purple onion, green onion, balsamic vinegar, basil, cilantro, salt and black pepper. Toss until combined. In a skillet over medium heat, add the corn, garlic and olive oil. Saute for 5-6 minutes or until the corn is tender. Remove the skillet from the heat and add the corn to the bowl.

Add the Dijon mustard to the bowl. Toss until combined and serve.

Tomato Zucchini Salad

Makes 8 servings

2 cups water
4 small zucchini, thinly sliced
1/8 tsp. salt
2 tomatoes, cut into wedges
2 slices purple onion, separated into rings
1 tbs. olive oil
1 tbs. balsamic vinegar
1 tsp. dried tarragon
1 tbs. Dijon mustard
1/2 tsp. salt
1/2 tsp. Tabasco sauce
1 garlic clove, minced
1 tbs. minced fresh parsley

In a sauce pan over medium heat, add the water, zucchini and salt. Bring the zucchini to a boil and cook for 3 minutes. Remove the pan from the heat and drain all the water from the pan. Rinse the zucchini in cold water. Pat the zucchini dry with paper towels.

In a serving bowl, add the zucchini, tomatoes and onion. In a glass jar, add the olive oil, balsamic vinegar, tarragon, Dijon mustard, salt, Tabasco sauce and garlic. Place a lid on the jar and shake until well combined. Pour the dressing over the salad. Toss until combined. Sprinkle the parsley over the top and serve.

Paprika Green Bean Salad

Makes 6 servings

6 cups fresh green beans
1/2 cup thinly sliced onions
1 cucumber, peeled and sliced
1/4 cup granulated sugar
1/4 cup vegetable oil
1/4 cup vinegar
1/2 tsp. paprika
1/4 tsp. salt
1/8 tsp. dried dill
1/8 tsp. celery seeds

Wash the green beans and trim the ends. Cut the green beans into 1" pieces. Add the water to a large sauce pan over medium heat. Bring the water to a boil and add the green beans. Cook for 10 minutes or until the green beans are crisp tender. Remove the pan from the heat and drain all the water from the green beans. Rinse the beans with cold water and drain all the water again.

Add the green beans, onions and cucumber to a large bowl. In a blender, add the granulated sugar, vegetable oil, vinegar, paprika, salt, dill and celery seeds. Process until smooth and combined. Pour the dressing over the vegetables in the bowl. Cover the bowl and chill for 2 hours before serving.

Green Bean Blue Cheese Salad

Makes 6 servings

6 cups fresh green beans, washed and ends trimmed
3 cups water
1 cup white wine vinegar
3/4 cup vegetable oil
1/2 cup diced red onion
2 tsp. grated lemon zest
6 cups lettuce leaves
1 cup crumbled blue cheese
1/2 cup chopped toasted walnuts

In a sauce pan over medium heat, add the green beans and water. Bring the green beans to a boil and place a lid on the pan. Cook about 8 minutes or until the green beans are tender. Remove the pan from the heat and drain all the water from the pan. Rinse the beans with cold water and drain all the water again. Refrigerate the green beans for 30 minutes.

In a large bowl, add the white wine vinegar, vegetable oil, red onion and lemon zest. Whisk until well combined and the oil is incorporated in the dressing. Add the green beans and toss until coated. Cover the bowl and chill for 3 hours.

Place the lettuce leaves on a serving plate. Using a slotted spoon, remove the green beans from the bowl and place on the lettuce. Sprinkle the blue cheese and walnuts over the top of the salad.

Hearty Cabbage Chowder

Makes 6 servings

3 tbs. melted unsalted butter
3 cups finely chopped cabbage
1 large potato, finely chopped
3 cups water
1 chicken bouillon cube
2 cups whole milk
1 cup shredded Swiss cheese
Salt and black pepper to taste

In a large sauce pan over low heat, add the butter, cabbage, potato and 1/2 cup water. Cook for 10 minutes or until the potato is tender. Using a fork, slightly mash the potato.

Add 2 1/2 cups water, chicken bouillon and milk to the pan. Stir until combined and simmer for 15 minutes. Add the Swiss cheese and stir until the cheese melts. Season to taste with salt and black pepper. Remove the pan from the heat and serve.

Hot Cream of Spinach Soup

Makes 6 servings

4 green onions, thinly sliced
4 tbs. unsalted butter
8 cups fresh spinach, washed and stems removed
4 cups chicken broth
3 tbs. all purpose flour
1/4 tsp. black pepper
Pinch of ground nutmeg
Pinch of dried basil
1 cup half and half
1 cup croutons, optional

In a dutch oven over medium heat, add the green onions and 1 tablespoon butter. Saute for 4 minutes. Add the spinach to the pan. Stir until combined and place a lid on the pan. Cook for 6 minutes or until the spinach is wilted and tender. Remove the pan from the heat.

Add the spinach to a blender. Add 1 cup chicken broth and process until smooth. Add 3 tablespoons butter to the dutch oven used to cook the spinach over medium heat. When the butter melts, stir in the all purpose flour. Stir constantly and cook for 2 minutes. Slowly add 3 cups chicken broth and stir until the soup begins to thicken.

Stir in the pureed spinach, black pepper, nutmeg and basil. Stir constantly and bring the soup to a boil. Reduce the heat to low and stir in the half and half. Stir constantly and cook only until the soup is thoroughly heated. Remove the pan from the heat. Spoon the soup into bowls and sprinkle the croutons over the top.

Spinach Potato Soup

Makes 7 cups

4 cups chicken broth
2 cups fresh spinach, washed and stems removed
6 green onions, diced
2 cups mashed potatoes
2 cups half and half
1/2 tsp. Tabasco sauce
1/2 tsp. black pepper

In a large sauce pan over medium heat, add the chicken broth. When the broth is boiling, add the spinach and green onions. Stir frequently and cook for 4 minutes. Remove the pan from the heat. Add the soup to a blender and process until smooth. Depending upon your blender, you may need to process the soup in batches.

Pour the soup back in the sauce pan. Stir in the mashed potatoes and whisk until smooth and combined. Reduce the heat to low and cook until the soup is thoroughly heated. Add the half and half, Tabasco sauce and black pepper to the pan. Stir until combined and cook only until the soup is hot. Do not let the soup boil once you add the half and half. Remove the pan from the heat and serve.

Cream of Mustard Green Soup

Makes 10 cups

40 cups fresh mustard greens or 4 1/2 lbs.
1 lb. cooked bone in ham slice
8 cups water
1/4 cup plus 1/3 cup unsalted butter
2 cups chopped green onions
2 cups chopped celery
1/3 cup all purpose flour
5 cups half and half
1/2 tsp. salt
1/8 tsp. Tabasco sauce

Wash the greens thoroughly and remove any large stems. Add the ham slice and water to a large dutch oven. Place the pan over medium heat and bring the water to a boil. Place a lid on the pan and reduce the heat to low. Simmer for 30 minutes.

Remove the ham from the liquid. You can finely dice the ham and serve with the soup or use for another recipe. Add the mustard greens to the pan. Stir until the greens begin to wilt. Stir occasionally and simmer the greens for 1 hour.

In a large skillet over medium heat, add 1/4 cup butter, green onions and celery. Saute for 5 minutes. Remove the skillet from the heat and add the butter, onion and celery to a food processor. Process until smooth.

In a large dutch oven, add 1/3 cup butter. When the butter melts, stir in the all purpose flour. Stir constantly and cook for 2 minutes. Reduce the heat to low. Continue stirring and add the half and half. Stir constantly and cook until the sauce thickens.

Add the mustard greens, onion puree, salt and Tabasco sauce to the pan. Stir until combined and the soup is hot. Do not let the soup boil. Remove the pan from the heat and serve.

Cream of Broccoli Soup

Makes 6 servings

4 cups water
2 cups chopped fresh broccoli
2 cups chopped ham
1 onion, chopped
1 potato, chopped
3 tbs. unsalted butter
1 1/2 tsp. dried basil
1 tsp. black pepper
1 chicken bouillon cube
1/2 tsp. dried thyme
1/2 tsp. salt
1 cup whole milk
3 tbs. grated Parmesan cheese, optional

In a large dutch oven over medium heat, add the water, broccoli, ham, onion, potato, butter, basil, black pepper, chicken bouillon, thyme and salt. Stir until combined. Bring to a boil and place a lid on the pan. Reduce the heat to low.

Simmer for 20 minutes or until the broccoli is tender. Using a hand blender, puree the soup. Add the milk and stir until combined. Cook only until the soup is thoroughly heated. Remove the soup from the heat and spoon into bowls. Sprinkle Parmesan cheese over the top if desired.

Cheese Broccoli Soup

Makes 8 servings

6 1/2 cups water
10 oz. pkg. frozen chopped broccoli
1 onion, chopped
8 oz. Velveeta cheese, cubed
2 tsp. black pepper
1/2 tsp. salt
1/2 tsp. garlic powder
1 cup whole milk
1 cup half and half
1/4 cup unsalted butter
1/2 cup all purpose flour

In a large sauce pan over medium heat, add 6 cups water and the broccoli. Bring to a boil and reduce the heat to low. Simmer for 10 minutes or until the broccoli is tender.

Add the Velveeta cheese, black pepper, salt and garlic powder. Stir constantly until the cheese melts. Do not let the soup boil once you add the cheese. Stir in the whole milk, half and half and butter. Stir constantly and cook until the soup is thoroughly heated.

In a small bowl, add the all purpose flour and 1/2 cup water. Whisk until well combined and add to the soup. Stir constantly and cook until the soup thickens and just begins to bubble. Remove the pan from the heat and serve.

Easy Broccoli Soup

Makes 4 cups

1/4 cup chopped onion
3 tbs. unsalted butter
3 tbs. all purpose flour
3 cups chicken broth
1 cup finely chopped fresh broccoli
1 bay leaf
1/2 cup whole milk
1/2 tsp. black pepper

In a sauce pan over medium heat, add the onion and butter. Saute for 5 minutes. Add the all purpose flour to the pan. Stir constantly and cook for 2 minutes.

Slowly whisk in the chicken broth, broccoli and bay leaf. Stir frequently and cook about 6 minutes or until the broccoli is tender. Reduce the heat to low and remove the bay leaf. Discard the bay leaf. Stir in the milk and black pepper. Cook only until the soup is thoroughly heated. Remove the pan from the heat and serve.

Artichoke Soup

Makes 4 servings

1 cup sliced green onions
1/4 cup chopped onion
2 tbs. melted unsalted butter
2 tbs. all purpose flour
14 oz. can artichoke hearts
14 oz. can chicken broth
1/4 tsp. black pepper
2 tbs. minced fresh parsley

In a large sauce pan over medium heat, add the green onions, onion and butter. Saute for 4 minutes. Sprinkle the all purpose flour over the onions. Stir constantly and cook for 2 minutes.

Drain the artichoke hearts but save the juice. Chop the artichokes into bite size pieces. Add the chicken broth, artichokes, artichoke juice and black pepper to the pan. Stir constantly and cook until the soup begins to thicken and bubbles. Remove the pan from the heat and spoon the soup into bowls. Sprinkle the parsley over the top before serving.

Cream Of Cauliflower Soup

Makes 2 quarts

1 large head cauliflower, cut into florets
2 cups chicken broth
2 tbs. instant chicken bouillon granules
2 cups half and half cream
2 cups whole milk
1 carrot, shredded
2 bay leaves
1/4 tsp. garlic powder
1/2 cup instant mashed potato flakes
2 cups shredded cheddar cheese, optional

In a large sauce pan over medium heat, add the cauliflower, chicken broth and chicken bouillon. Bring to a boil and place a lid on the pan. Reduce the heat to low and simmer for 20 minutes or until the cauliflower is tender. Remove the pan from the heat. Mash the cauliflower with a fork or potato masher.

Add the cauliflower and liquid to a 4 quart slow cooker. Add the half and half cream, milk, carrot, bay leaves and garlic powder. Stir until combined. Set the temperature to low. Cook for 3 hours. Stir in the mashed potato flakes. Cook for 30 minutes. Remove the bay leaves from the soup and discard. Stir in the cheddar cheese if desired. Cool for 5 minutes before serving.

Creamy Cabbage Chowder

Makes 8 servings

4 cups shredded green cabbage
2 cups sliced carrots
3 cups diced potatoes
1 tbs. salt
1/2 tsp. black pepper
1/2 tsp. granulated sugar
2 cups water
2 tbs. unsalted butter
4 cups whole milk

In a large sauce pan over medium heat, add the cabbage, carrots, potatoes, salt, black pepper, granulated sugar and water. Bring the vegetables to a boil and reduce the heat to low. Simmer for 12 minutes or until the vegetables are tender.

Add the butter and whole milk to the pan. Stir constantly and cook until the butter melts and the chowder is thoroughly heated. Do not let the soup boil once you add the milk. Remove the pan from the heat and serve. We like to serve this chowder with saltine crackers and slices of roast beef on the side.

Asparagus Soup

Makes 4 servings

8 cups fresh asparagus
1 tbs. unsalted butter
1 tsp. vegetable oil
1/4 cup minced onion
1/4 cup chopped fresh parsley
1 tsp. ground coriander
1 tbs. all purpose flour
2 1/2 cups chicken broth
2 tsp. lemon juice
Black pepper to taste
1/2 cup whole milk

Remove the woody ends from the asparagus and trim off the tough scales on the stalks. Add the asparagus to a large sauce pan over medium heat. Cover with water and cook about 8 minutes or until the asparagus is tender. Remove the pan from the heat and drain all the water from the pan. Cut the asparagus into 2" pieces and set aside for the moment.

In a large saucepan over medium heat, add the butter and vegetable oil. When the butter melts, add the onion, parsley and coriander. Stir constantly and cook for 3 minutes. Reduce the heat to low and sprinkle the all purpose flour over the pan. Stir constantly and cook for 1 minute. Add the chicken broth to the pan. Stir constantly and cook until the soup thickens and bubbles.

Remove the pan from the heat and add the asparagus. Add the soup to a blender container. Puree until smooth. Add the lemon juice and black pepper to taste. Add the soup back to the sauce pan and add the milk. Stir constantly and cook until the soup is thoroughly heated. Remove the pan from the heat and serve.

Creamy Asparagus Soup

Makes 2 quarts

1/2 cup chopped onion
1 cup sliced celery
3 garlic cloves, minced
3 tbs. melted unsalted butter
2 cans cut asparagus, 14 oz. size
14 oz. can chicken broth
1 tsp. white vinegar
1 tsp. salt
1/2 tsp. black pepper
1/4 tsp. cayenne pepper
1/2 tsp. dried basil
1 cup whole milk
1/2 cup sour cream, optional

In a dutch oven over medium heat, add the onion, celery, garlic and butter. Saute the vegetables for 6 minutes. Add the asparagus with liquid, chicken broth, white vinegar, salt, black pepper, cayenne pepper and basil to the pan. Stir until well combined. Reduce the heat to low and simmer for 10 minutes.

Remove the pan from the heat and pour the soup into your blender container. Depending upon the size of your blender, you may need to puree the soup in batches. Process the soup until smooth.

Add the pureed soup back to the dutch oven over low heat. Add the milk and cook only until the soup is thoroughly heated. Remove the soup from the heat and serve. Spoon a dollop of sour cream over each serving if desired.

Butternut Squash Soup

Makes 6 servings

2 tsp. olive oil
1 cup chopped onions
1 tsp. minced garlic
1 tbs. grated fresh ginger
1/2 tsp. ground cumin
6 cups peeled & cubed butternut squash
2 cups chicken broth
1 1/2 cups carrot juice
1/4 cup frozen pineapple juice concentrate
1 tsp. grated orange zest
1/2 tsp. salt
1/4 tsp. black pepper

In a large dutch oven over medium heat, add the olive oil. When the oil is hot, add the onions and garlic. Saute for 3 minutes. Add the ginger and cumin to the pan. Saute for 30 seconds.

Add the butternut squash, chicken broth, carrot juice, pineapple juice concentrate, orange zest, salt and black pepper to the pan. Stir until combined and bring the soup to a boil. Reduce the heat to low and place a lid on the pan. Simmer for 15 minutes or until the squash is tender.

Remove the pan from the heat. Using a hand blender, puree the soup. Serve hot.

Carrot Red Pepper Soup

Makes 4 servings

1 red bell pepper
1 lb. carrots, sliced
1 onion, chopped
2 tbs. dry long grain rice
2 tbs. butter
4 1/2 cups chicken broth
2 cups water
1/3 cup orange juice
4 1/2 tsp. minced fresh dill
2 tsp. grated orange zest
1/2 tsp. salt
1/2 tsp. dried marjoram
1/2 tsp. dried thyme
1/2 tsp. dried rosemary
1/2 tsp. rubbed sage
1/4 tsp. black pepper

Place the red bell pepper on a baking sheet. Preheat the oven to the broiler position. Turn the pepper frequently so all sides char evenly. Broil about 5 minutes or until the pepper is blistered and charred. Remove from the oven and place the pepper in a bowl. Cool for 20 minutes. Remove the skin from the pepper. Remove the stem and seeds from the pepper.

In a large sauce pan over medium heat, add the carrots, onion, rice and butter. Saute for 5 minutes. Add the chicken broth, water, orange juice, dill, orange zest, salt, marjoram, thyme, rosemary, sage and black pepper. Stir until combined and bring to a boil. Reduce the heat to low and place a lid on the pan. Simmer for 20 minutes or until the carrots are tender. Remove the pan from the heat.

Add the red bell pepper to the soup. Cool the soup for 5 minutes. Using a hand blender, puree until smooth and combined.

Broccoli Sauce

Serve this sauce over hot pasta or any meat. It is an easy and tasty way to sneak vegetables into your diet.

Makes 2 cups

1 1/2 cups boiling water
3 cups chopped fresh broccoli florets
1 chicken bouillon cube
2 tbs. melted unsalted butter
1/4 cup chopped onion
2 tbs. all purpose flour
3/4 cup whole milk
1/2 tsp. dried dill
1/2 tsp. black pepper

In a sauce pan over medium heat, add 1 cup boiling water and the broccoli. Bring to a boil and place a lid on the pan. Simmer for 6 minutes or until the broccoli is tender. Remove the pan from the heat and drain off all the water.

Add the broccoli, 1/2 cup water and chicken bouillon cube to a blender. Process until smooth. In a large sauce pan over medium heat, add the butter and onion. Saute for 3 minutes. Sprinkle the all purpose flour over the onion. Stir constantly and cook for 1 minute. Add the milk to the pan. Stir constantly and cook until the sauce thickens and bubbles.

Add the broccoli, dill and black pepper to the pan. Stir constantly and cook only until the soup is thoroughly heated. Remove the pan from the heat and serve.

Green Pepper Saute

This side dish is delicious or it can be served over pasta, rice or beans.

Makes 4 servings

3 large green bell peppers, cut into 1/2" slices
1 cup sliced celery
1 cup thinly sliced onion
1 garlic clove, minced
2 tbs. olive oil
15 oz. can tomato sauce
1/2 tsp. dried basil
Salt and black pepper to taste
1/2 cup crushed garlic croutons

In a large skillet over medium heat, add the green bell peppers, celery, onion, garlic and olive oil. Saute for 6 minutes. Add the tomato sauce and basil to the skillet. Saute for 8 minutes or until the vegetables are tender. Remove the skillet from the heat and season to taste with salt and black pepper. Sprinkle the garlic croutons over the top and serve.

You can substitute a 15 oz. can diced tomatoes for the tomato sauce if desired. The tomatoes with seasonings added are really good in this dish.

Vegetable Pasta Sauce

This is so easy to make and delicious over pasta, rice or Italian bread.

Makes 4 servings

2 cans diced tomatoes, 15 oz. size
15 oz. can whole tomatoes
1 1/2 cups sliced fresh mushrooms
1 red bell pepper, diced
1 green bell pepper, diced
1 yellow squash, cut into 1/4" slices
1 zucchini, cut into 1/4" slices
6 oz. can tomato paste
4 green onions, sliced
2 tbs. dried Italian seasoning
1 tbs. chopped fresh parsley
3 garlic cloves, minced
1 tsp. salt
1 tsp. dried red pepper flakes, optional
1 tsp. black pepper

Add all the ingredients to a 5 quart slow cooker. Do not drain the tomatoes. Stir until combined. Set the temperature to low. Cook for 6 hours or until the sauce thickens to your taste.

CHAPTER INDEX

Green Vegetable Side Dishes

Green Vegetable Side Dishes cont'd

Beer Braised Collard Greens, 23
Simple Collard Greens, 23
Wine & Bell Pepper Collards, 24
Bourbon Bacon Collards, 24
Braised Endive and Green Peas, 25
Cooked Escarole, 25
Skillet Swiss Chard, 26
Blue Cheese Coleslaw, 26
Mexicorn Ranch Slaw, 27
Chinese Slaw, 27
Texas Corn Slaw, 28
Sesame Slaw, 28
Old Fashioned Coleslaw, 29
Coleslaw with Tomatoes, 29
Chili Coleslaw, 30
Lemon Butter Cabbage, 30
Orange Cranberry Cabbage, 31
Cabbage Saute, 31
Stir Fry Cabbage, 32
Cabbage and Dumplings, 32
Smothered Cabbage Wedges, 33
Cabbage Stroganoff, 34
Cheese Scalloped Cabbage, 34
Cabbage Vegetable Skillet, 35
Bubbling Cabbage, 35
Wilted Cabbage, 36
Country Style Cabbage, 36
German Red Cabbage, 37
Artichoke Hearts with Lemon, 37
Garlic Green Beans, 38
Basil Green Beans, 38
Green Beans & New Potatoes, 39
Green Bean Saute, 39
Creole Green Beans, 40
Roasted Green Beans With Sun Dried Tomatoes, 40
Herb Green Beans, 41
Barbecue Green Beans, 41
Blue Cheese Green Beans, 42
Blue Cheese Bacon Green Beans, 42
Green Beans with Buttered Pecans, 43
Green Beans with Pepper Strips, 43
Cheesy Green Beans, 44
Spanish Green Beans, 44
French Quarter Green Beans, 45
Lemon Green Beans, 45

Lemon Dill Green Beans, 46
Holiday Green Beans, 46
Zucchini Green Beans, 47
Butter Garlic Green Beans, 47
Grilled Asparagus & New Potatoes, 48
Asparagus in Squash Rings, 48
Roasted Orange Ginger Asparagus, 49
Asparagus Mushroom Saute, 49
Jeweled Asparagus, 50
Marinated Asparagus, 50
Sweet and Sour Asparagus, 51
Asparagus Supreme, 52
Asparagus in Basil Sauce, 52

Squash, Cauliflower, Tomatoes & Other Vegetables

Spinach Stuffed Squash, 54
Twice Baked Squash, 54
Mexican Summer Vegetables, 55
Curry Butternut Squash, 55
Zucchini Bake, 56
Roasted Fennel And Summer Squash, 56
Acorn Squash With Raisin Spice Sauce, 57
Maple Glazed Squash, 57
Bacon Squash Saute, 58
Sauteed Squash & Tomatoes, 58
Zucchini Latkes, 59
Zucchini Parmesan Toss, 59
Pesto Veggie Stacks, 60
Vegetarian Paella, 61
Grilled Vegetable Packets, 62
Grilled Teriyaki Vegetable Packets, 62
Braised Leeks, 63
Caramelized Onions, 63
Roasted Leeks, Potatoes & Carrots, 64
Carrots & Broccoli With Orange Browned Butter, 64
Ginger Lime Carrots, 65
Roasted Italian Vegetables, 65
Roasted Root Vegetables, 66
Pepper Parsnip Fries, 66
Roasted Parsnips & Apples, 67
Parsnip Sweet Potato Patties, 67
Roasted Beets, 68
Ginger Orange Beets, 68
Roasted Turnips With Honey Butter, 69
Sorghum Glazed Turnips, 69
Tomato Corn Risotto, 70
Smoky Grilled Corn, 71
Corn Stuffed Peppers, 71
Cheese Stuffed Peppers, 72
Southwest Sweet Corn And Zucchini, 72
Poached Corn, 73
Fresh Corn Medley, 73
Garden Stir Fry, 74
Fresh Tomatoes With Parsley Pesto, 74
Bean Stuffed Tomatoes, 75
Onion Topped Tomatoes, 75
Orange Marjoram Carrots, 76
Glazed Julienned Carrots, 76
Carrots & Pearl Onions, 77
Creamed Mushrooms, 78

Garlic Goat Cheese Stuffed Mushrooms, 78
Bacon & Cheese Stuffed Mushrooms, 79
Sauteed Portobello Mushrooms, 79
Burgundy Mushrooms, 80
Goat Cheese Basil Grilled Bell Peppers, 80
Bacon Fried Okra, 81
Okra Skillet, 81
Cauliflower With Red Pepper Sauce, 82
Cauliflower With Raspberry Vinaigrette, 82
Curry Potatoes, Cauliflower & Green Peas, 83
Cheesy Slow Cooker Cauliflower, 84
Maple Vegetable Medley, 85

Casseroles

Soups & Salads

Soups & Salads cont'd

ABOUT THE AUTHOR

Lifelong southerner who lives in Bowling Green, KY. Priorities in life are God, family and pets. I love to cook, garden and feed most any stray animal that walks into my yard. I love old cookbooks and cookie jars. Huge NBA fan who loves to spend hours watching basketball games. Enjoy cooking for family and friends and hosting parties and reunions. Can't wait each year to build gingerbread houses for the kids.

Manufactured by Amazon.ca
Bolton, ON